ZELENSKY

ZELENSKY

The Unlikely Ukrainian Hero Who Defied Putin and United the World

ANDREW L. URBAN AND CHRIS McLEOD

Foreword by Rebekah Koffler

Regnery Publishing

WASHINGTON, D.C.

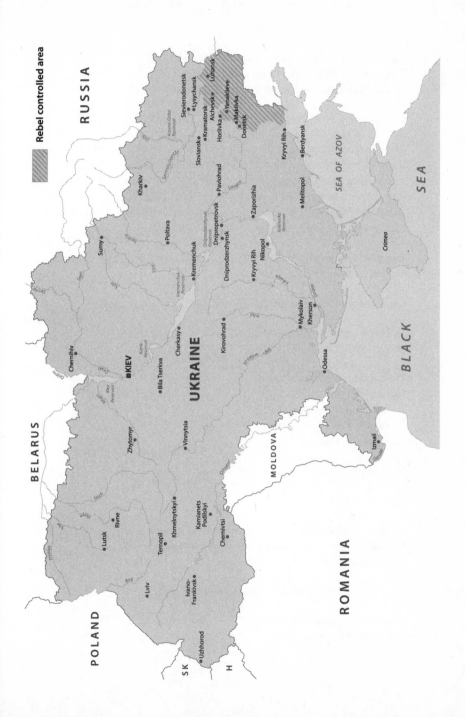

Copyright © 2022 by Andrew L. Urban and Chris McLeod
Foreword copyright © 2022 by Rebekah Koffler
Published by arrangement with Wilkinson Publishing Pty. Ltd.

Interior design by Michael Bannenberg and Spike Creative

Cataloging-in-Publication data on file with the Library of Congress

ISBN: 978-1-68451-378-9
eISBN: 978-1-68451-379-6

Published in the United States by
Regnery Publishing
A Division of Salem Media Group
Washington, D.C.
www.Regnery.com

Manufactured in the United States of America

10 9 8 7 6 5 4 3 2 1

Books are available in quantity for promotional or premium use.
For information on discounts and terms, please visit our website:
www.Regnery.com

Ukraine map image used under license from Shutterstock

Published simultaneously in Australia and New Zealand by
Wilkinson Publishing

CONTENTS

FOREWORD

"I need ammunition, not a ride!"

In an age where genuine heroism is so rare, President of
Ukraine Volodymyr Zelensky's *cri de coeur* echoed around the
world. Zelensky could have fled — Washington had offered
him a safe passage out of Kyiv — but he chose to fight for his
country, slim though the chances of victory were.

Days earlier, Russia's Vladimir Putin had launched a brutal
war on Ukraine, eager to bring the country back under
Moscow's yoke. The Russians closed in quickly on Kyiv,
hoping to "decapitate" the Zelensky government — that is, kill
Zelensky — and install a puppet regime.

But Zelensky was not deterred, even after multiple
assassination attempts conducted by Putin's hit squads. He
rose to meet the opposition and stood firm, displaying a
courage that many thought no longer existed in today's world.

Virtually unknown outside of his native Ukraine before the
war, Zelensky has earned respect from his fellow Ukrainians
and adoration from Western elites and ordinary citizens alike.
He has displayed an indomitable spirit in a deeply unfair

fight. The Russian military far outclasses the Ukrainian, but Ukrainian soldiers and volunteers have shown that spirit still counts for something on the battlefield. We haven't seen this ferocious a will in Europe to push back an enemy since the Russians defended Stalingrad against German invaders in World War II.

The 44-year-old entertainer turned servant of the people Zelensky has measured up to his adversary, the staunch spymaster and Judo expert Putin. Putin, who cut his teeth as a KGB operative alongside the most brutal and devious the old Soviet Union had to offer, has used all the tricks he learned from those KGB days. And at times, Zelensky has still outmaneuvered him.

Unlike Putin, who doesn't use email and is stuck in the pre-internet era, Zelensky has proven himself an adept fighter on new, digital frontiers. Zelensky won his election in 2019 through a savvy social media campaign. In the current crisis, he has shown the world that he is a social media maestro, leading a concerted YouTube, Facebook, Instagram, and Twitter effort with the grace and skill of a conductor directing his orchestra. An entertainer who is used to reading the audience, Zelensky knows what the West wants to hear. He has upstaged Putin in the information warfare department.

This talent for crafting narratives has paid dividends. Zelensky has won over the hearts of the West's policy planners and politicians, who are eager to support the charismatic

Ukrainian. Western intellectuals clamor to give Zelensky the "No Fly Zone" he wants, even if it means dragging the United States and NATO into a "shooting war" with Russia that would almost certainly escalate into a nuclear conflict. Zelensky may have won the West's heart, but has that come at the expense of its head?

We have all come to see President Zelensky as a hero, but some of his decisions are not as straightforward as we in the West think. Zelensky, much like Ukraine itself, is filled with contradictions. The Ukrainians are a freedom-loving people but among the most corrupt in Europe. And while Zelensky declares his love for his nation, he failed to protect it from a destructive assault that may lead to scores of civilian deaths, the erasure of its borders, and the annihilation of its culture.

Is Zelensky brave or reckless? Zelensky must know that Putin will never allow Ukraine to join the Western political or military orbit without a fight. For the past 20 years, Putin has planned to reverse the outcome of the Cold War. In his mind, losing Ukraine to Western influence is not an option.

Still, Zelensky often chooses to poke the bear. With thousands of Russian soldiers amassed on his border, Zelensky made open appeals for NATO membership. Now, with Russian boots on Ukrainian soil, he goads Putin to escalate his assault, even daring the Russian to carpet-bomb Kyiv. To paraphrase a famous saying about Vietnam, Zelensky may allow his country to be destroyed in order to save it.

Is Zelensky a Ukrainian George Washington, ready to forfeit his own life to set his country on the path towards freedom? Or is his bravado driven by a performer's ego and sense of drama? Perhaps a bit of both, and the balanced account that follows will help you decide what to make of this new star of geopolitics.

Rebekah Koffler
Author of *Putin's Playbook: Russia's Secret Plan to Defeat America*

INTRODUCTION

As an actor and comedian, Volodymyr Zelensky made people laugh.

As President of Ukraine, a country under siege from Russia, Volodymyr Zelensky addressed the European Parliament where he was given a standing ovation and reduced a translator to tears.

President Zelensky's plea for support from Europe in the face of deadly bombardment from Vladimir Putin's Russia was no laughing matter.

The man who once played the piano with his genitals for five minutes to howls of laughter pleaded for Europe and the West to stand by his still fledgling democracy as the Russian military laid siege to Ukrainian cities, killing civilians in the process.

There was one big stumbling block to the US-backed NATO alliance joining in — fear of starting World War III.

President Joe Biden said he would defend NATO to the point of World War III, but that he wouldn't risk touching off a wider conflict by fighting Russia in Ukraine and ruled out establishing a no-fly zone that Russia would regard as an act of war.

President Biden told Americans: "The idea that we're going to send in offensive equipment and have planes and tanks and trains going in, American pilots and American crews, just understand. Don't kid yourself, no matter what you all say, that's called World War Three, okay?"

One of Putin's pretexts was to put down Ukraine's supposed move along the path to Nazism.

His action was said to be aimed at protecting citizens in the newly recognized (by Russia) regions in the Donbas and *"demilitarizing"* and *"de-Nazifying"* Ukraine itself.

The Nazi pretext just didn't seem to hold water. To begin, far-right candidates garnered just 2% of the Ukrainian vote in 2019 elections.

More likely it was about trying to renew the old Union of Soviet Socialist Republics. And of course, Ukraine's resources would be worth having — iron ore, manganese, coal, bauxite, natural gas and petroleum among them. Also, Putin wasn't keen on a neighbor joining the North Atlantic Treaty Organization (NATO) and its close ties with the West, the United States in particular. As a condition of ending the Russian advance, he demanded NATO refuse membership to Ukraine. It was increasingly unlikely Ukraine's application would proceed anyway.

One of President Zelensky's first tweets (social media now a major instrument in waging war) as Russia launched its invasion on February 24, 2022 was: "Russia treacherously attacked our state in the morning, as Nazi Germany did in #2WW years. As of today, our countries are on different sides of world history. (Russia) has embarked on a path of evil, but (Ukraine) is defending itself & won't give up its freedom no matter what Moscow thinks."

They are not the words of a Nazi-sympathizer.

Zelensky would hardly identity with the Hitler regime whose aim was extermination of Jews. He was born into a Jewish family and was the first Jewish President of his country.

The history of Russia and Ukraine have been linked for centuries, since Kyiv (Kiev as used in Russia) became the capital of the ancient state of Rus. They also have closely related languages, and many people in the two countries have family links.

In the early 20th century, the two nations and nearby Belarus formed the Slav core of the communist Soviet Union.

Ukraine and Russia stayed aligned after the 1991 dissolution of the Soviet Union, but as the 21st century began, Ukraine sought closer ties with Europe.

And that particularly irked the Russian President.

The writing was on the wall for further aggression in 2014 when Ukraine's pro-Russian government was toppled, leading Russia to annex Ukraine's Crimea Peninsula and make clear its support for the separatist insurgents in Ukraine's east.

To many observers in Europe, it was only a matter of time until Putin ordered the full invasion of Ukraine. Putin had always described Ukrainians and Russians as one people, ironic when his military started killing Ukrainian civilians as the much-anticipated invasion began when tanks emblazoned with the letter "Z" rolled into Ukraine.

President Zelensky told German newspaper *Die Zelt*: "The invasion was no surprise to me, but the brutality was. What the Russian soldiers are doing to the civilians is more than I can comprehend. The bombs they're dropping on apartment buildings. The missile systems they're using to shell residential areas. Those are war crimes."

On March 1, 2022, President Zelensky made an impassioned address to the European Parliament: "We want our children to live on. It seems to me that this is fair. Yesterday, 16 children died. And again, President Putin will say that this is some kind of an 'operation,' and that they are bombing only our military infrastructure. Where are our children? At what military plants do they work? Which rockets do they operate? Maybe they drive our tanks? You killed 16 children!"

Putin upped the ante: He warned of consequences for Western countries interfering and put his nuclear attack capability on alert. The West (and NATO) however would not put "boots on the ground" in fear of starting World War III.

President Zelensky told the European parliament: "We are simply fighting for our land and our freedom, and believe me, despite the fact that all the big cities of our state are now under blockade, no one will penetrate our freedom and state. Believe me. Every square today, whatever it is called, will be referred to as Freedom Square. In every city of our state. Nobody will break us, we stand strong, we are Ukrainians."

Just what would the end game be? There was no confidence around the world that there would be a peaceful solution. The popular belief was that the end would come with Ukraine — or parts of it — falling under Russian rule, either by capitulation or concession. No one was predicting a peaceful Russian retreat.

The possibility of a short war dissipated when Ukraine offered a level of resistance Russia appeared not to expect and a drawn-out conflict was considered most likely, even spreading into neighboring countries.

Another possibility that had some backers was the ousting of President Putin in Russia, though how that might occur would depend on a massive uprising or even assassination.

Assassination was something on the mind of Ukrainians — reports said there were at least 12 assassination attempts on President Zelensky's life in the first three weeks of the conflict.

The comedian remained defiant. He wasn't in this for laughs.

CHAPTER 1

CHURCHILL IN A T-SHIRT

The invasion of Ukraine by Russia was barely a week old as the populace took shelter from the bombardment, some in their basements, some in the metro stations — and some in the familiar embrace of self-preserving humor.

President Putin and his driver were on their way to Kyiv in a car when all of a sudden they hit a pig near a farmhouse, killing it instantly.

Putin told his driver to go up to the farmhouse and explain to the owners what had happened. About one hour later Putin sees his driver staggering back to the car with a bottle of Horilka (Ukrainian vodka) in one hand, a cigar in the other and his clothes all ripped and torn.

"What happened to you?" asked Putin.

"Well, the farmer gave me the Horilka, his wife gave me a box of cigars and their 19-year-old and 21-year-old daughters made mad passionate love to me simultaneously."

"My God, what did you tell them?" asks Putin.

The driver replies, "I'm president Putin's driver, and I just killed the pig."

Dozens if not hundreds of such jokes riddled the internet, a perfectly apt phenomenon for a country whose President was a successful Jewish comedian in the years before being sworn in on May 20, 2019, with over 72% of the vote. Jews have a sharpened belief in the saving grace of humor, acquired over millennia as God's chosen punching bags.

On January 25, 2022, less than three years after taking office, Volodymyr Zelensky celebrated his 44th birthday, a month before the invasion. Refusing offers to be whisked out of Ukraine to safety, Zelensky's stature on the world stage grew even faster than Putin's stature shrank. "The fight is here; I need antitank ammo, not a ride," he said in a video he posted on twitter on the morning of February 26.

This guerrilla President — quickly labelled 'Churchill in a T-shirt' — broadcast courage to his people and admonished the West. In a televised address late on Friday, March 4, 2022, Ukraine time, he said, "Today there was a NATO summit, a weak summit, a confused summit, a summit where it was clear that not everyone considers the battle for Europe's freedom to be the number one goal.

"Today, the leadership of the alliance gave the green light for further bombing of Ukrainian cities and villages, having refused to set up a no-fly zone."

The President then took to Twitter, calling on world leaders to "not watch, but help."

The day before, Zelensky's emotional plea inspired a standing ovation from members of the European parliament, and brought interpreters to tears, as ABC News reported:

Ukraine's President Volodymyr Zelensky has urged the European Union to prove that it stands with Ukraine in its war with Russia, a day after signing an official request to join the bloc.

"We are fighting to be equal members of Europe. I believe that today we are showing everybody that is what we are," an emotional Mr Zelensky told an emergency session of the European parliament via video link.

"Nobody is going to break us." (*See Chapter 4 for transcript.*)

[It was irony on a grand scale: there was Zelensky, successfully urging and inspiring his nation, whose flag is half yellow, to bravery.]

EU politicians, many wearing #standwithUkraine T-shirts bearing the Ukrainian flag, others with blue-and-yellow scarves or ribbons, gave Mr Zelensky a standing ovation.

The speech came hours after Mr Zelensky submitted an application to the European Union to grant Ukraine immediate membership.

In an open letter, Lithuania, Latvia, Estonia, the Czech Republic, Bulgaria, Slovakia, Slovenia, and Romania expressed support for Ukraine's swift entry.

Russia's war on Ukraine is now in its sixth day, with a miles-long convoy of Russian tanks and armored vehicles inching closer to the Ukrainian capital and fighting intensifying on the ground.

Russian artillery hit the main central square in Ukraine's second-largest city Kharkiv, and other civilian targets, Ukrainian authorities said.

Mr Zelensky has remained in Kyiv to rally his people against the invasion.

"Do prove that you are with us. Do prove that you will not let us go. Do prove that you are indeed Europeans and then life will win over death and light will win over darkness," he said in Ukrainian, bringing the English interpreter to tears.

A German interpreter translating the speech on live TV abruptly stopped before she broke down into tears.

Mr Zelensky accused Moscow of resorting to "terror" tactics in Europe's largest ground war since World War II.

He said 16 children had been killed around Ukraine on Monday, and mocked Russia's claim that it was only going after military targets.

"Where are the children? What kind of military factories do they work at? What tanks are they going at?" he asked.

From inside a bunker, Mr Zelensky told reporters he was open to dialogue, but Russia needed to stop bombarding

Ukraine before any ceasefire talks.

"Stop bombarding people first and start negotiating afterwards," he said.

"Everybody has to stop fighting and to go to that point from where it was beginning."

He also called for security guarantees if NATO members were not ready to admit Ukraine to the bloc.

On day 14 of the invasion, Zelensky gave an interview to Ben C. Solomon of VICE News, reiterating his and his country's defiance. He also reflected on how he saw NATO at that time.

"First of all. I want security guarantees from NATO. I only know one thing. As of today, it looks like this. The current situation is a betrayal of our ideals and trust. We are grateful to NATO countries for giving us weapons and other things. But we just wanted to be equal. That's it. But it turns out that equality costs a lot, and not everybody gets it."

"What is your message for young people?" asked Solomon.

"I can't come up with a message for them... these people are independent, free and very strong. They will endure everything, overcome everything, go through fire and water. It's only thanks to those people that our world exists and there is justice. What do I want to wish them? They are awesome I hope they don't change."

"Can you make a compromise with Putin? Can you trust Putin?" Solomon asked Zelensky in the interview. "Trust? Oh no. I trust only my family."

"How can you make a deal with somebody you don't trust then?"

"We have to. We have to. Because this war had to stop. Only dialogue, and only dialogue with him, the President of Russia. Russia is fighting against Ukraine. They came to our land, to our houses, to our children. We didn't invite them. But they're here now. They are here."

"What would be your message to President Vladimir Putin right now?"

"Right now, stop the war, begin to speak."

It cannot be any clearer: 141 countries of the world condemned Russia for its invasion of Ukraine as illegitimate in a vote at the UN General Assembly. And all 141 countries had done nothing to stop Russia continuing to break international law. But Putin got a good finger wagging… Addressing the UN membership, Secretary-General António Guterres stated that "the fighting in Ukraine must stop."

He continued: "I must say, President Putin: In the name of humanity bring your troops back to Russia. In the name of humanity do not allow to start in Europe what could be the worst war since the beginning of the century, with consequences not only devastating for Ukraine, not only tragic for the Russian Federation, but with an impact we cannot even foresee in relation to the consequences for the global economy in a moment when we are emerging from the COVID [pandemic] and so many developing countries absolutely need to have space for the recovery which would be very, very difficult, with the high prices of oil, with the end of exports of wheat from Ukraine, and with the rising interest rates caused by instability in international markets. This conflict must stop — now. Thank you very much."

The UN resolution was passed at a special meeting of the General Assembly called because of a lack of unanimity of the permanent members, so that the UN's Security Council fails to:

"... exercise its primary responsibility for the maintenance of international peace and security in any case where there appears to be a threat to the peace, breach of the peace, or act of aggression."

Unlike a Security Council resolution, a General Assembly resolution does not have the potential to become legally binding. As the UN puts it, they're "considered to be recommendations. But it does have strong symbolic value and reflects international opinion."

Tough talking UN Secretary-General Antonio Guterres said the resolution sent a message "loud and clear" to Russia. "End hostilities in Ukraine now. Silence the guns now," he said. "Open the door to dialogue and diplomacy now. The territorial integrity and sovereignty of Ukraine must be respected in line with the UN Charter. We don't have a moment to lose." That was many, many lost moments ago…

Incapable of passing a resolution to do something to halt Russia's invasion by force in the Security Council where Russia and China have veto rights, the UN proved itself as useful as that proverbial ashtray on a motorbike.

NATO allies rejected Ukraine's request to set up and enforce a no-fly zone over Ukraine, saying that it would lead to a larger, more devastating conflict across Europe. "We are not part of this conflict, and we have a responsibility to ensure it does not escalate and spread beyond Ukraine," NATO Secretary-General Jens Stoltenberg told a news conference on Friday in Brussels, echoing statements made by White House officials several days earlier (and subsequently) about a no-fly zone.

It was argued in a column in *The Spectator Australia* (March 8, 2022): "The Russian invasion force is acting illegally in a sovereign state; Ukraine is a democracy which is asking, begging, for military assistance to defend itself against a more powerful aggressor. If that assistance endangers the respondents, what hope for any peace at the hands of Putin?

"The major powers — the US, UK, Germany, France — joined by other willing nations, should be able to form a 'pop up' United Nations-like force that diffuses the target among themselves and does what the UN should be doing. Under the operational command of a tested military leader, that 'international peace force' would patrol the no-fly zone and perhaps extend its operations to assisting the Ukrainian ground forces."

And there was another possibility, canvassed in a letter to *The Australian* (March 9) from reader Glenn Simpson. He wrote:

> *A possible solution to the Ukraine crisis would be a UN-sanctioned peacekeeping force, backed by a Security Council resolution, but such a resolution would be vetoed by the Russian Federation. However, the UN Charter provides that the Soviet Union has a permanent seat on the Security Council, not the Russian Federation, which is only one successor state representing only part of the former Soviet Union and has succeeded to that seat by courtesy and general agreement. That courtesy should be withdrawn, and the seat on the Security Council declared by the General Assembly to have lapsed with the demise of the Soviet Union. Then a fresh resolution can be put to the Security Council requiring the Russian Federation to withdraw its troops, or face a combined UN force such as fought in Korea in 1949–52.*

Earlier, on February 24, the eve of the invasion, Zelensky's video address (translated below) demonstrated his determination for averting war:

"Today I initiated a phone call with the president of the Russian federation. The result was silence. Though the silence should be in Donbas. That's why I want to address today the people of Russia. I am addressing you not as a president, I am addressing you as a citizen of Ukraine. More than 2,000 km of the common border is dividing us. Along this border your troops are stationed, almost 200,000 soldiers, thousands of military vehicles. Your leaders approved them to make a step forward, to the territory of another country. And this step can be the beginning of a big war on European continent.

"We know for sure that we don't need the war. Not a Cold War, not a hot war. Not a hybrid one. But if we'll be attacked by the [enemy] troops, if they try to take our country away from us, our freedom, our lives, the lives of our children, we will defend ourselves. Not attack, but defend ourselves. And when you will be attacking us, you will see our faces, not our backs, but our faces.

"The war is a big disaster, and this disaster has a high price. With every meaning of this word. People lose money, reputation, quality of life, they lose freedom. But the main thing is that people lose their loved ones, they lose themselves.

"They told you that Ukraine is posing a threat to Russia. It was not the case in the past, not in the present, it's not going to be in the future. You are demanding security guarantees from NATO, but we also demand security guarantees. Security for Ukraine from you, from Russia and other guarantees of the Budapest memorandum.

"But our main goal is peace in Ukraine and the safety of our people, Ukrainians. For that we are ready to have talks with anybody, including you, in any format, on any platform.

The war will deprive [security] guarantees from everybody — nobody will have guarantees of security anymore. Who will suffer the most from it? The people. Who doesn't want it the most? The people! Who can stop it? The people. But are there those people among you? I am sure.

"I know that they [the Russian state] won't show my address on Russian TV, but Russian people have to see it. They need to know the truth, and the truth is that it is time to stop now, before it is too late. And if the Russian leaders don't want to sit with us behind the table for the sake of peace, maybe they will sit behind the table with you. Do Russians want the war? I would like to know the answer. But the answer depends only on you, citizens of the Russian Federation."

When the threat of invasion hung like a black cloud over Ukraine and Western leaders were jittery, Zelensky's now famous, sarcastic but misunderstood jive about the anticipated timing of Russia's move ('February 16') was buried in his February 14 address to the Unity of Ukrainian Society:

[As translated by the Ukrainian Government]

Great people of a great country! I am addressing you at this tense moment.

Our state is facing serious external and internal challenges that require responsibility, confidence and concrete actions from me and each of us.

We are being intimidated by the great war and the date of the military invasion is being set again. This is not the first time.

The war against us is being systematically waged on all fronts. On the military one, they increase the contingent around the border. On the diplomatic one, they are trying to deprive us of the right to determine our own foreign policy course. On the energy one, they limit the supply of gas, electricity and coal. On the information one, they seek to spread panic among citizens and investors through the media.

But our state today is stronger than ever.

This is not the first threat that the strong Ukrainian people have faced. Two years ago, we, like the rest of the world, looked confused in the eyes of the pandemic. However, we united and with clear systemic steps practically defeated it. In this difficult time, the strong Ukrainian people have shown their best qualities - unity and the will to win.

Unlike the pandemic two years ago, today we clearly understand all the challenges we face and what to do about them. We are confident, but not self-confident. We understand all the risks. We are constantly monitoring the situation, working out different scenarios, preparing decent responses to all possible aggressive actions.

We know exactly where the foreign army is near our borders, its numbers, its locations, its equipment and its plans.

We have something to respond with. We have a great army. Our guys have unique combat experience and modern weapons. This is an army many times stronger than eight years ago.

Along with the army, Ukrainian diplomacy is at the forefront of defending our interests. We have managed to gain diplomatic support from almost all leaders of the civilized world. Most of them have either already visited and supported Ukraine, or will do so in the near future. Today, everyone recognizes that the security of Europe and the entire continent depends on Ukraine and its army.

We want peace and we want to resolve all issues exclusively through negotiations. Both Donbas and Crimea will return to Ukraine. Exclusively through diplomacy. We do not encroach on what's not ours, but we will not give up our land.

We are confident in our Armed Forces, but our military must also feel our support, our cohesion and our unity. The foothold of our army is the confidence of their own people and a strong economy.

We have formed sufficient reserves to repel attacks on the hryvnia exchange rate and our financial system. We will not ignore any industry that will need government support. As it happened the other day with airlines. And evidence of this is a stable hryvnia exchange rate and open skies.

An important front of defense is the objective coverage of the situation by the domestic media. And now I want to address our Ukrainian journalists. Some of you sometimes have to perform the tasks of media owners. Most of them have already fled their own country.

Work for Ukraine, not for those who fled. The fate of the country today depends on your honest position.

And now I want to address not those who stayed with Ukraine and in Ukraine, but those who left it at the most crucial moment. Your strength is not in your money and planes, but in the civic position you can show. Return to your people and the country due to which you got your factories and wealth. Today, everyone passes a real test for a citizen of Ukraine. Pass it with dignity. Let everyone understand for whom Ukraine is really the Homeland, and for whom it is just a platform for money making.

I address separately all representatives of the state: civil servants, people's deputies of all levels who have fled the country or plan to do so. The people of Ukraine have entrusted you not only to govern the state, but also to protect it. It is your direct duty in this situation to be with us, with the Ukrainian people. I urge you to return to your homeland within 24 hours and stand side by side with the Ukrainian army, diplomacy and people.

We are told that February 16 will be the day of the attack. We will make it the Day of Unity. The relevant decree has already been signed. On this day, we will hoist national flags, put on blue and yellow ribbons and show the world our unity.

We have one great European aspiration. We want freedom and are ready to fight for it. 14,000 defenders and civilians killed in this war are watching us from the sky. And we will not betray their memory.

We all want to live happily, and happiness loves the strong ones. We have never known what it is to give up and we are not going to learn that.

Today is not just Valentine's Day. It is the day of those in love with Ukraine. We believe in our own strength and continue to build our future together. Because we are united by love for Ukraine, united and unique. And love will win. Yes, now you may think it's darkness all around. But tomorrow the sun will rise again over our peaceful sky.

Love Ukraine!

We are calm! We are strong! We are together! Great people of a great country.

———————————

Support for him and Ukraine was universal. For example, Australian Prime Minister Scott Morrison held a private phone call with Zelensky where they discussed ways Australia could assist Ukraine further. The Prime Minister tweeted on March 5 that he also "condemned" Russia's actions on behalf of all Australians: "Just spoke with Ukrainian President Zelensky. He thanked Australia for our military & humanitarian support & extensive sanctions. We discussed ways we could assist further. I praised Ukraine's courage against Russia's aggression & condemned Russia's actions on behalf of us all."

MailOnline's Dan Wootton perfectly captured the feelings of the brand new, spontaneous, and global Zelensky Admiration Society in his March 1 column:

> Oh, how they sniggered.
>
> When famed physical comic Volodymyr Zelensky was elected President of Ukraine in 2019 with over 70 percent of the vote on an anti-corruption mandate versus his pro-Russia opponent, the mainstream media treated his elevation as, well, a bit of a joke.
>
> "Ukrainians are waking up this morning and discovering that the last few months were not a dream. They really have elected a man who currently stars in a TV series as the president — as the country's next real president," the BBC sneered in the hours after his historic election, having previously described him as "clueless".
>
> Commentators were even harsher.
>
> The famous Ukrainian writer Oksana Zabuzhko wrote: "I hear an offscreen laugh of scriptwriters who have conjured all this plot for stupid Ukrainians."
>
> No one is laughing at Zelensky now.
>
> The Ukrainian president has proven he's nothing like our craven modern politicians who don't give a damn about the folk they represent; so much so that he's prepared to die alongside his fellow Ukrainians to defend the capital Kyiv against the near certain upcoming onslaught from Vladimir Putin.

When the 44-year-old received an offer of evacuation from US authorities this weekend, with Russian troops continuing to encircle Kyiv, he delivered a line straight from a Hollywood action movie: "We need ammo, not a ride."

Who believes that would be the response from a snivelling Macron, pampered Trudeau or braindead Biden in the same circumstances?

It certainly wasn't the response by Afghanistan's former president Ashraf Ghani who jumped on a US helicopter full of cash out of Kabul last year before it was even officially confirmed the Taliban were nearby.

No wonder Boris Johnson remarked after a recent phone call with Zelensky: "Jesus, that guy is brave."

Because be in no doubt that the lives of Zelensky, his screenwriter wife Olena Zelenska and two children, daughter Aleksandra, 17, and son Kiril, nine, are now unquestionably on the line.

They're Putin's "number one targets", with a death order being given to 400 brutal Russian mercenaries already operating in the city, who have express orders from the Kremlin to assassinate Zelensky, according to *The Times* today.

In a twist no scriptwriter could have predicted, Zelensky — once a comic star in Russia, the country now out to kill him — has become the world's heroic leading man.

It's Zelensky's career in showbiz — he also won the local version of *Strictly Come Dancing* and is the Ukrainian voice of

Paddington — that has helped Ukraine win the propaganda effort hands down.

His powerful oratory via official channels and social media has already changed the course of this conflict.

Indeed, some of his speeches over the past week have been so powerful that TV translators have had to stop talking because they can't contain their emotions.

There was his savage taunt to Putin: "When you attack us, you will see our faces, not our backs."

Or his address to the Munich Security Conference on February 19, where he helped the world wake up to the coming horrors by saying: "When a bomb crater appears in a school playground, children have a question: 'Has the world forgotten the mistakes of the 20th century?' Indifference makes you an accomplice."

And when the Russian disinformation campaign suggested Zelensky had fled the capital, he simply took his mobile phone to the streets and made a selfie video to reassure his people he wasn't going anywhere.

"We're all here. Our military is here. Citizens in society are here. We're all here defending our independence, our country — and it will stay this way," he insisted.

Then there's the video call with EU leaders — reluctant to enter the conflict — soon after the Russian invasion, where he warned them: "This might be the last time you see me alive."

These are all the sorts of powerful lines that could have been uttered by his character Vasyl Petrovych Holoborodko in the TV series *Servant of the People*, which ended in 2019, where his character, a teacher, became the president after a rant he made about corruption went viral after being posted on the internet by his students.

As politicians around the world, from Sleepy Joe Biden to Mr Blackface Authoritarian Justin Trudeau, become more of a joke AFTER they take office, Zelensky has morphed from comedian to statesman over the course of just a few weeks.

Compare Zelensky's rhetoric with that of Britain's MI6 chief Richard Moore.

Moore has spent the crisis talking about gay rights for some unknown reason, unfathomably tweeting: "With the tragedy and destruction unfolding so distressingly in Ukraine, we should remember the values and hard-won freedoms that distinguish us from Putin, none more than LGBT+ rights."

WTAF? No wonder Putin and China's Jinping continue to treat us with such disdain.

But in hardman Zelensky — dressed in his green military fatigues, showing off a body once toned on *Dancing With The Stars* — Putin has encountered a far tougher opponent.

His authenticity and ability to speak directly to Russians in their language has convinced many to support his cause, helping lead to large illegal anti-war protests on the streets of Moscow and St Petersburg.

Zelensky's personal story has also helped repudiate Putin's

propaganda campaign that the first illegal invasion of a sovereign country by a superpower in 80 years is all down to ridding Ukraine of Nazis.

He is from a Jewish family and his grandfather Semyon Ivanovych was the only one of his four brothers to survive the Holocaust, with the others all killed by Nazis.

As an incredulous Zelensky has pointed out: "How can I be a Nazi? Explain it to my grandfather, who went through the entire war in the infantry of the Soviet army and died a colonel in an independent Ukraine."

Zelensky — most famous before the war for starring in that infamous phone call with Donald Trump that resulted in the US president's political impeachment in the house — had been down in the polls before Putin decided to go to war with Ukraine, having been unable to stamp out the country's rampant corruption as promised.

His close relationship with the billionaire oligarch Ihor Kolomoyskyi raised eyebrows and critics believe he surrounded himself with too many pro-Russian, anti-Western advisers who may have wrongly convinced him that war could be averted, despite intelligence from the UK and US to the contrary.

But none of that matters now.

Leaders are judged by history on their actions in wartime.

And Zelensky's approach has been highly effective, garnering tougher sanctions, more military supplies and piling the pressure on the West to man the hell up and stop appeasing Putin.

His history-making news clips posted directly to social media have seen his followers soar, with over three million on Twitter and 12 million on Instagram.

Like Donald Trump before him, he has the authenticity so lacking in our modern-day politicians, who seem to have become paranoid, scripted robots.

Biden couldn't even get through a press conference on the conflict without breaking into inappropriate smirks, for God's sake.

Zelensky is rightly now a global hero, but whether he survives the war is impossible to predict, given Putin — who runs a well-oiled international killing machine — wants him dead.

Perhaps what's most heart-warming is that Zelensky never needed to enter politics; he had national superstardom, millions in the bank, luxury villas and a highly successful career in Russia, until he donated money to help support the Ukrainian army in 2014.

Zelensky once said: "You don't need experience to be president. You just need to be a decent human being."

And it's that innate decency which is why he'd rather die alongside his citizens in Kyiv than cut and run on a US helicopter.

I pray that this inspirational figure can lead Ukraine out of this quagmire — the world will be a better place for it.

Indeed, a "decent human being" may well deliver better outcomes than experience in politics.

But, of course, it wasn't just his stirring speeches that gave him a hero's glow; it was that defiant stand against the Russian bully, that action which spoke louder even than his accented Churchillian words.

Comparing his country's fight against Russia to the British war effort against Nazi Germany, he told the British House of Commons via video link: "You didn't want to lose your country when Nazis wanted to take your country," as he invoked Winston Churchill and said Ukraine "will continue fighting for our land, whatever the cost. We will fight in the forests, the fields, the shores and in the streets."

(Fuelling Churchill memories... a couple of weeks later, the Prime Ministers of Poland, Czech Republic, and Slovenia covertly took a train into Kyiv to meet with Zelensky, reminiscent of US President Roosevelt's flight to meet Churchill in Casablanca.)

Zelensky was speaking in an informal sitting as the first non-member to address the Chamber (usually world leaders speak in the Royal Gallery or Westminster Hall) and appeared on large screens over MPs' heads at 5pm on March 8, 2022.

For all the applause and promises of support across the political board that followed his short speech (and a standing ovation that replaced taking a stand with a fist Putin would understand), his central and unwavering call for the protection of a no-fly zone remained a no-go. It wasn't even mentioned in reply speeches by either PM Boris Johnson or the Opposition's Keir Starmer. (But an embargo on Russian energy was finally declared by the US soon after.)

But more than his repeated appeals to the West, it was those video clips of him as literally "the man in the street" when the street was deadly dangerous that showed a clear case of the moment making the man.

The resume of his life prior to his Presidency was not out of the Ukrainian ordinary for a successful entertainment performer.

Nor was his decision to adopt the name of his TV show as the name of his political vehicle: Servant of the People. In Western culture, it may seem flippant. In the culture of Eastern Europe, and in a country where politicians had been anything but servants of the people, it seemed apt, a promise. It struck a chord, as they say. (Western politicians should resist feeling smug: they, too, could take on that promise as a personal mission.) Zelensky also adopted the show's storyline: actor/comedian becomes popular President.

The party was created in March 2018 by the founders of Kvartal 95, the TV production company. A year after its creation, Zelensky gave an interview to Der Spiegel, in which he declared that he "wanted to bring professional, decent people to power" because he "would really like to change the mood and timbre of the political establishment, as much as possible". Old hands in politics would have laughed behind his back — especially in Ukraine, one of the most corrupt countries in Europe. But they didn't have the majority of the votes… Nor did they feature as favorites in opinion polls, like Zelensky did.

Many will remember the headlines when he was elected: "Ukraine election: Comedian Zelensky wins presidency by landslide" as the BBC had it. Was it his wonderful humor that made people laugh when nothing else was funny? Or was it his old fashioned (romantic?) notion that politics should be clean? It wasn't his looks: neither ugly nor handsome, he looks… well, average, with a pleasant if nondescript face, pointed chin and neat hair. He married Olena Kiyashko in 2003; they went to the same school but didn't meet until later, and she joined Kvartal 95 as a writer. They have a daughter, Oleksandra, born in July 2002 and a son, Kyrylo, born in January 2013.

In the golden years of Hollywood, Zelensky would have been played by Jimmy Stewart. These days, probably Tom Hanks… In the media rush amidst the invasion, *The Economist* portrayed Zelensky as the boy from the rough neighborhood who stared down all his adversaries:

Zelensky was born in 1978 in Kryvyi Rih, a Soviet-looking industrial city in the southeast of Ukraine, a center of iron mining and metallurgy.

His favorite film was *Once Upon a Time in America*.

To survive among the town's knife-wielding gangs, you had

to have a sense of humor, chutzpah and a posse that had your back. Zelensky had all these things in abundance.

He burst on to the political scene in 2019. He was not a candidate of Ukrainian-speaking western Ukraine or of the Russian-speaking east. Instead, he rejected the linguistic, historical and ethnic split that has long been exploited both by Ukrainian politicians and by the Kremlin.

Partly as a result, he has brought the country closer together than it has been for years. Zelensky was driven by neither nationalism nor ideology. Nor was he a revolutionary. He was an everyman.

"Zelensky is fighting like a lion and the whole of Ukraine with him," says Sevgil Musaeva, a Ukrainian journalist and the editor of *Ukrainska Pravda*, the country's main online news site.

Some news reports in February and March 2022, named the Private Military Company (PMC) Wagner Group as one of the teams seeking to assassinate Zelensky on behalf of Putin. This is an international operation active since 2014, under its granite faced leader Dmitry Valeryevich Utkin, who named the unit in honor of the German composer... a nod to Utkin's passion for the Third Reich. Previously, Utkin had been a lieutenant colonel and brigade commander of Special Forces of the Main Directorate of the General Staff of the Russian Armed Forces.

In December 2016, Utkin was photographed with Putin at a Kremlin reception given in honor of those who had been awarded the Order of Courage and the title Hero of the Russian Federation.

But the man ultimately behind Wagner and its source of finance is said to be Yevgeny Prigozhin, aka "Putin's Chef", a reference to his closeness to Putin and his extensive catering interests.

Russian and some Western observers believe that the organization does not actually exist as a private military company (owned by "Putin's Chef") but is a disguised branch of the Russian Ministry of Defence (MoD) that ultimately reports to the Russian government.

Sure enough, Wagner personnel — of whom there are now estimated to be some 6,000 — are trained at the Russian MoD facility Molkino, near Molkin village, in Krasnodar Krai. Described as a holiday camp for children, these barracks are not officially linked to the MoD.

Wagner employees were among the "little green men" who participated in the Russian takeover of Crimea in 2014 and assisted Russian separatists in Eastern Ukraine attempting to secede from the country, according to Weapons and Warfare. "Due to the group's involvement in conflicts in these countries, Wagner has been repeatedly targeted for sanctions by the US government. In 2016, the US Treasury Department placed sanctions on Prigozhin via executive order for his 'extensive business dealings with the Russian Ministry of Defence' and for building bases to support Russian military actions in Ukraine."

Early in 2020, Erik Prince, founder of the Blackwater Private Military Company, sought to provide military services to the Wagner Group in its operations in Libya and Mozambique, according to *The Intercept.* By March 2021, Wagner PMCs were reportedly also deployed in Zimbabwe, Angola, Guinea, Guinea Bissau, and possibly the Democratic Republic of Congo.

In late 2019, according to Wikipedia, a so-called Wagner code of honor was revealed that lists ten commandments for Wagner's PMCs to follow. One is to protect the interests of Russia always and everywhere, to value the honor of a Russian soldier, to fight not for money, but from the principle of winning always and everywhere.

Since foiling three separate attempted assassinations (thanks to betrayal by anti-war elements within Russia's Federal Security Service), the Ukraine Government has made plans to ensure a smooth transition to a successor if such an attempt is successful in future.

On March 7, Zelensky (perhaps recklessly) issued a defiant video of himself disclosing his location, saying he is "not afraid of anyone and not hiding" and reiterating that he plans to stay and fight.

Nobody in the political establishments of the world nor among the public thinks the invasion is anything but a Putin solo flight.

Farida Rustamova of the BBC's Russian service, in a piece written for Substack, described the demeanor of Putin's closest advisors days before the invasion:

> As a former security officer, [Putin] always wants to take everyone by surprise… We saw this during an emergency extended meeting of the Security Council three days before the war. The stammering of Foreign Intelligence chief Sergei Naryshkin, the disorientation of the deputy head of the Kremlin administration, Dmitry Kozak, and the anxious face of Moscow Mayor Sergei Sobyanin, were more than eloquent.

> The most influential people in Russia sat in front of Putin like schoolchildren before a teacher who suddenly announced a test. And this meeting after all wasn't even about the war, they discussed only the recognition of the self-proclaimed DPR [Donetsk People's Republic] and LPR [Luhansk People's Republic].

Rustamova, as author and journalist Matt Taibbi reported on his TK News website, went on to quote a source close to the discussions describing the reaction among the officials: "They carefully pronounced 'p—ts'." The missing word is *pizdets*, not an easy word to translate — like a more profane and dire version of *clusterfuck*. She noted that "according to him, the mood in the corridors of power is altogether not rosy, many are in a state of stupor." Another source told her, "Nobody is thrilled, many understand that this is a mistake, but out of duty they come up with rationalizations for themselves in order to make it work in their heads."

Even Putin's fiercest critics have always seen him as cold, calculating, and pragmatic, writes Taibbi. That soon changed. *Bloomberg*'s Leonid Bershidsky, a former *Moscow Times* co-worker, tweeted:

> *If Putin does attack, the presumption of his rationality, which has been part of my analysis of his actions for the last 23 years, not just the past few weeks, will need to be thrown out the window.*

The prospect of a Putin victory quickly faded. "As the Russo-Ukrainian War takes a darker turn it is important to emphasize this essential point: This is a war that Vladimir Putin cannot win, however long it lasts and however cruel his methods," wrote Lawrence Freedman, emeritus professor of war studies at King's College London, in Homeland Security Newswire. But he also noted: "If only for reasons of prudence, we must still assume that the Russians will be more successful in bringing the weight of their military strength to bear."

Freedman captured the essence of the issue: "From the start, the Russian campaign has been hampered by political objectives that cannot be translated into meaningful military objectives. Putin has described a mythical Ukraine, a product of a fevered imagination stimulated by cockeyed historical musings. His Ukraine appears as a wayward sibling to be rescued from the "drug addicts and Nazis" (his phrase) that have led it astray. It is not a fantasy that Ukrainians recognize. They see it as an excuse to turn their country into a passive colony and this they will not allow."

Indeed, Admiral Sir Tony Radakin, the chief of the UK defence staff, told *The Times* (March 8) that Moscow had "got itself into a mess" and that its invasion was "not going well".

The Times reported that as many as 11,000 Russian soldiers had been killed in the fierce fighting, according to the latest approximate figures published by the Ukrainian armed forces on Sunday March 6. An estimated 44 aircraft, 285 tanks, 985 armored vehicles, 109 artillery systems and 60 fuel tanks have also been destroyed. Admiral Radakin said the Kremlin had lost more troops in a week than the UK did in 20 years in Afghanistan. He also said that the morale of the invading soldiers had been knocked so badly that some had abandoned the convoy destined for Kyiv to camp in the forest.

Déjà vu? *The Nineteen Days* (Heinemann) is 'a broadcaster's account of the Hungarian revolution'. That broadcaster was my father, George R. Urban. The book was written in the immediate aftermath of the revolution, my father sitting at his trusty typewriter in a Hampstead cottage, while I floated around in childish joy at my new-found freedom as a refugee in London. The following excerpts document a significant time in the 1956 Revolution: Point of No Return.

One pertinent reason for the poor fighting spirit of the Soviet tank crews was their supply position. They were expected to be able to live on the land or buy food in the shops. Faced by a hostile population, they could not do either. It did not take them long to discover that only arms and ammunition could buy the precious articles and that the men to contact were the freedom fighters. It is difficult to overestimate the part which the Russian's foods shortage played both in undermining their own loyalties and raising the hopes of the population. In the capital and later in other cities and industrial centers, guns and even tanks were freely offered to the freedom fighters and the population in exchange for a few loaves of bread. The evidence that comes from a young worker from Miskolc is typical of many similar cases:

I was on my way to X when I saw two Russian tanks come up behind me. I was carrying two loaves of bread and about a kilo and a half of sausages. The Russians in the tanks must have seen that I had food in my basket. They stopped and one of them got out. He carried an automatic. He knew a little Hungarian as he had been in the country for some time. As far as I could make out, he asked me to give them my loaf and offered his tank in exchange. He looked completely starved. I took a loaf from my bag and cut a chunk for them. We talked for a while. Then he began to ask me for the rest of the food I was carrying. As they had the guns and I had nothing, I gave them all the food I had. Then I said to him, "Give me a gun." He gave me his automatic with 14 bullets. When they got the food, he and another one who had joined him, began to weep. They told me they would take me home. I said there was no need to do that. I would go on my own. The first Russian then told me that they would like to come with me. They would do any work as long as they were allowed to stay in Hungary. If they were sent home, they would be liquidated. Of course, I couldn't take the tank. I didn't know how to drive it, and even if I did, what would I do with a tank single-handed? So I said to them, "Look, boys, I don't want your ruddy tank. All I wanted was a gun and I got that." But they didn't think it was a good idea to stop there talking to me. So, I said goodbye to them and walked off.

Zelensky is the direct opposite of Putin, politically and personally. For example, it was Zelensky (on March 5) who expressed sympathy for the thousands of young Russian soldiers, "children really, 18, 19, 20," dying in the conflict. Ten days later, Zelensky was offering them "a chance to survive."

"Russian conscripts! Listen to me very carefully," Zelensky said, during an address, according to his Presidential office. "Russian officers! You've already understood everything. You will not take anything from Ukraine. You will take lives. There are a lot of you. But your life will also be taken. But why should you die? What for? I know that you want to survive.

"Therefore, I offer you a choice. On behalf of the Ukrainian people, I give you a chance. Chance to survive. If you surrender to our forces, we will treat you the way people are supposed to be treated. As people, decently. In a way you were not treated in your army. And in a way your army does not treat ours. Choose!"

No wonder he is embraced by the global community, whereas Putin is reviled.

Zelensky's Presidential campaign was conducted largely on social media (sound familiar?) and he succeeded in unseating incumbent President Petro Poroshenko, a well-known oligarch.

Several members of the Presidential Administration were former Zelensky colleagues from his production company, Kvartal 95, including Ivan Bakanov, appointed deputy director of the Ukrainian Secret Service (Americans will recognize this familiar jobs-for-the-boys routine from their observations of Washington DC).

Like all politicians and especially leaders, Zelensky had (and no doubt still has) his critics. Some were critical of the way his moves to reduce the influence of oligarchs helped centralize his own power. The question yet to be answered is how did he use (or intend to use) that power?

As the Russians pushed towards Kyiv, most of the US political class swung behind Zelensky. But not all. The US response to the Russian invasion has divided the old guard of the GOP — including figures like Senate Minority Leader

Mitch McConnell (R-Ky.) and Sen. Lindsey Graham (R-S.C.), who have called for heavy US involvement in the conflict — from more populist-leaning newcomers like Rep. Madison Cawthorn (R-N.C.), Senate candidate J.D. Vance, and conservative Fox News commentator Tucker Carlson, who have demanded that the US stay out of the conflict.

In March, footage emerged of Cawthorn saying: "Remember that Zelensky is a thug, remember that the Ukrainian government is incredibly corrupt and it is incredibly evil and it has been pushing woke ideologies. It really is the new woke world empire."

Karl Rove, a Republican strategist, first mentioned Cawthorn's remarks while speaking to a crowd in Asheville recently, before WRAL-TV published footage of Cawthorn speaking.

According to Joseph Lord reporting in the *Epoch Times*, Cawthorn provided no examples of thuggish or evil behavior as evidence to support his assertion. But the assertion became a political football around the Russian invasion of Ukraine. "Let's be clear," said state Sen. Chuck Edwards (R-NC) on Twitter. "The thug is Vladimir Putin. We must unite as a nation to pray for President Zelensky and the brave people of Ukraine who are fighting for their lives and their freedom."

"I do not understand how anyone in American public office could call Zelensky a 'thug' while Ukraine is under such vicious assault," said Michele Woodhouse in a statement posted to her campaign website. "Conservatives in my district are terrified that we will lose this republican seat to a leftist Biden democrat if Cawthorn somehow wins the nomination." (Cawthorn is a first term Representative.)

Cawthorn has made clear that he does not approve of Russia's actions either. "The actions of Putin and Russia are disgusting," Cawthorn said on Twitter on March 10, the same day the footage was released. "But leaders, including Zelensky, should NOT push misinformation on America."

The report did not mention any examples of what Cawthorn termed misinformation.

The *Epoch Times* reported that Cawthorn's office didn't respond to a request for comment.

In a statement to a news outlet, a spokesman for Cawthorn explained his position further. Cawthorn "supports Ukraine and the Ukrainian President's efforts to defend their country against Russian aggression, but does not want America drawn into another conflict through emotional manipulation," the spokesman said. Again, without supporting examples.

Ironically enough, one of Zelensky's stated ambitions was to end the protracted conflict with Russia and he wanted to engage Putin in direct dialogue. Obviously, it was a popular, if unfulfilled, goal.

The Ukrainians threw out their Russia-friendly President, Viktor F. Yanukovich, without guns, in early 2014. The Maidan Square-centered protest, which had begun at the end of 2013, was maintained in the face of armed official and brutal unofficial forces. It is superbly captured in the 102-minute documentary, *Winter on Fire: Ukraine's fight for Freedom* (2015).

The film, directed by Evgeny Afineevsky and written by Den Tolmor, shows in vivid detail the sheer determination, courage and resourcefulness of the Ukrainians. Putin should have watched the film before stating his objective of breaking the spirit of the Ukrainian people. They had no guns but they did have guts, and they had the will to free themselves from the cruel rule of communist puppet Yanukovich. There is security camera footage of him fleeing at dawn...

Astonishing footage of the fighting, rousing speeches of the protesters, heartbreaking scenes of brutality and sacrifice are woven together with the words of the participants themselves, speaking to camera. It is effectively making us an embedded observer.

And so are we embedded observers of the 2022 Russian invasion, with cameras recording it for now and for posterity. We watch in our homes as a war criminal in the Kremlin murders Ukrainians and dictates to the world. Only Zelensky, it seems, is really standing up to him, as best he can.

CHAPTER 2
UNSOCIAL MEDIA

Russia's attack — war, although the Russians didn't use that word — on Ukraine was not just being fought on the ground and from the air.

The use — or not — of social media became a critical point of influence for both Ukraine and Russia, the former for enlisting support and the latter for stifling and controlling the flow of information. Both are functions of propaganda, good and bad.

USA Today noted: "There's no question the Ukraine invasion is a social media war — the world's first. Many TV interviews are with Ukrainians who are garnering large social media followings. TikTok is filled with video clips of after-bombing scenes and bomb shelters. They are shot on smartphones by citizens and shared directly with the world, bypassing traditional media outlets."

Ukraine sympathizers have weighed in heavily, too.

Believing, correctly on the evidence, that Russian people were not being told the full story, a Norwegian computer expert and his team created a website enabling anyone to send an email about the war in Ukraine to up to 150 Russian email addresses at a time.

Whether Russians believed the information or not would be unclear, but they were at least hearing the views of Ukrainians — and others — to which they would otherwise not have access.

The messages, estimated at 22 million within the first few days of their use, carried the subject line, *Ya vam ne vrag* — "I am not your enemy."

With Russian access to other social media platforms controlled, the standard message appeared in Russian with an English translation. It read: "Dear friend, I am writing to you to express my concern for the secure future of our children on this planet. Most of the world has condemned Putin's invasion of Ukraine."

The message urged Russians to reject the war in Ukraine and find the truth about the invasion from non-state news services.

These emails and the welter of social media posts were the modern-day version of the World War II leaflet drops.

A member of the Norwegian team made contact with a 35-year-old woman in St Petersburg who first asked to be removed from the mailing list. The Norwegian made further contact. He said: "She told me she wasn't sure what was going on in the conflict and wanted to know more. She said there was a lack of news coming out of Europe and she wanted to read about it all but didn't know how to get through the blocks on websites."

Indicative of Russian knowledge of what was really going on, another team member received a reply from an unknown Russian who argued strongly that she was wrong and it was Ukraine that was killing innocent people which is why "this special operation is a necessary measure."

Russians themselves are finding ways to circumvent the bans on popular social media platforms.

Reports said many Russians had used a virtual private network (VPN) with an encrypted connection between their devices and a remote server. Such a server could be anywhere in the world, so in theory could link to sites blocked in Russia.

Technology experts warned that many pro-Russian posts contained old and fake footage.

Twitter launched a new privacy-protected version of its site for Russians to access it more easily.

Meanwhile, Russian prosecutors moved to designate Mark Zuckerberg's Meta, the owner of Facebook, Instagram and WhatsApp, as an "extremist organization," which would permit harsher crackdowns on users and content providers.

President Zelensky was aware of the impact of social media. He joined Twitter in April 2019 and three years later had 5.2 million followers.

Weeks into Russia's invasion the President had 14.1 million followers on Instagram.

There is little doubt his followers played no small part in his landslide win in 2019.

It was also clear President Zelensky understood the importance of public opinion in the West.

He posted videos to social media and tweeted statements calling for help and expressing resolve to the extent he became a global hero, virtually, without personal appearances.

He addressed governments in the West, updated and reassured his citizens and taunted Russians in their own country, all via social media.

His campaigns and social media posts played a huge part in mobilizing worldwide protests against the Russian action and in support of Ukraine.

His regular Tweets updated followers on his discussions with world leaders. Two Tweets from March 12:

> *"I spoke with Olaf Scholz, Emmanuel Macron (Germany and France). We talked about Russian aggression and the prospect of peace talks. We must stop repressions against civilians: asked to assist in the release of the captive mayor of Melitopol and Local figures."*

> *"Had a substantial conversation with POTUS (President Biden). Gave him the assessment of the situation on the battlefield, informed about the crimes of Russia against the civilian population. We agreed on further steps to support the defence of Ukraine and increased sanctions against Russia."*

Ukraine's social media campaign was to present at home and abroad an image of unified resistance to Russian aggression.

Social media arms in Ukraine published content showing alleged combatants threatening to kill Russians, instructions on how to make Molotov cocktails, Russian helicopters being shot down and civilians apparently confronting Russian soldiers.

Zelensky's personal accounts (access is sometimes flaky) have regularly published "selfie" videos to lay to rest rumors that he fled the country or surrendered to the Russians.

He said in a video posted to Instagram: "I'm staying in Kyiv... on Bankova Street," not afraid to reveal his location. He used his mobile phone to film out the window to show the street across from the presidential palace, recognizable to Ukrainian viewers.

In one of his regular addresses to his followers and Russians listening in he said: "Our office, Monday. You know we used to say Monday is a hard day. There is a war in our country, so every day is Monday, and now we are used to the fact that every day and every night are like that... I am in Kyiv. My team is with me... We are not afraid of you."

Most of his statements were translated by his office for wider consumption.

When the Russians bombed a maternity hospital in southern Ukraine, the President immediately took to social media, posting words and pictures.

He tweeted: "Mariupol. Direct strike of Russian troops at the maternity hospital. People, children are under the wreckage. Atrocity! How much longer will the world be an accomplice ignoring terror? Close the sky right now! Stop the killings! You have power but you seem to be losing humanity."

In a video posted online, he said: "Today is the day that defines everything. It defines who is on which side. Children's hospital. A maternity hospital. What did they threaten the Russian Federation with?

"Were there little nationalists there? Were pregnant women going to shoot missiles at Rostov? Did someone in that maternity hospital offend Russian-speaking people? Was it the 'denazification' of the hospital? This is beyond atrocities already," he said.

His wife, Olena, also shared an emotional statement and videos on Instagram about the bombing.

Her videos showed the debris, as well as some people trying to help, and a few people could be seen leaving the scene.

Russia's embassy in London first stamped a giant "FAKE" over tweeted photos of the atrocity in Mariupol, insisting the hospital only housed neo-Nazi radicals.

When commentators pointed to photos of a heavily pregnant woman fleeing with blood dripping from her face, the embassy claimed the woman was a "beauty blogger" with "some very realistic make-up." There was a possibility that woman was a beauty consultant who was in the hospital at the time, about to give birth.

Facebook and Twitter eventually removed the embassy's posts.

Later reports said the woman had given birth but both she and the baby died after surgery.

Pro-Russia accounts on social media are aimed at convincing people not to believe news reports about Ukrainians suffering and dying.

They spread false claims that media outlets have been showing fake footage of Ukrainian "crisis actors" — happy, healthy people playing the role of terrified or deceased war victims for the cameras.

Many of the dubious assertions often emanate from Russian embassies in Europe.

The Russian embassy in Geneva often shared unsupported claims about Ukraine on Twitter, including allegations a Ukraine paramilitary group was using Mariupol hospital patients and staff as human shields.

Another report emanating from Russia claimed that Zelensky fled to Poland and had lied to Ukrainians about his presence in the capital. Such reports often were picked up by state outlets of friendly countries, such as Iran.

Russia's flow of demonstrably false reports prompted Meta, Twitter, Google and others to restrict state-backed Russian media outlets such as RT and Sputnik.

In retaliation, Russia made it illegal for the media to contradict President Putin's official line on the war (though that word was not used) and blocked Facebook and Twitter.

The social media war took an even more serious tone when leaked emails revealed Facebook and Instagram users in some countries would be allowed to call for violence against Russians and the death of Vladimir Putin on these platforms.

Britain's *Independent* newspaper reported that Meta was temporarily changing its hate speech policy for posts regarding the war in Ukraine for the countries involved and most neighboring European countries.

The *Independent* said internal emails told content moderators that posts calling for the death of Putin or Belarus president Alexander Lukashenko would be allowed, in a change to the company's rules on violence and incitement.

The emails said calls for violence against Russians were acceptable when the post was clearly talking about the invasion of Ukraine. Calls for violence against Russian soldiers would be considered a proxy for the Russian military — but this would not extend to prisoners of war.

CHAPTER 3
LIE, DENY, JUSTIFY

Russia's approach to criticism about its invasion of Ukraine followed the pattern used for decades by autocratic regimes to deal with controversial actions.

There will be lies, denials or dubious justifications, or all of the above.

President Putin and Vladimir Solovyov, a Russian journalist, television presenter, writer and propagandist known for anti-Ukraine statements, falsely claimed Ukraine struck first, and an invasion was necessary to "de-Nazify" the country. (The 2019 election produced only 2% of the vote for far-right candidates, according to reports, and hardly sufficient to suggest Ukraine was following a path to Nazism.)

"Today is the day on which the righteous de-Nazification of Ukraine begins. A most important day, a day which decides the course of our history," Solovyov said on his YouTube channel, Solovyov LIVE.

Media technology sites issued warnings about pro-Russian posts that included footage from video games and old military exercises as fake examples of Ukraine attacking Russia.

"There are even two examples of videos on Twitter

today that are actually from war-themed video games, something Russian state media has previously tried to do on multiple occasions," Gizmodo noted on the Thursday after Russia launched its invasion.

Another stark example was Russia's insistence that it was not targeting civilians in Ukraine. Yet on March 9, A Russian air strike hit a children's and maternity hospital. An enraged President Zelensky tweeted: "Direct strike of Russian troops at the maternity hospital. People, children are under the wreckage. Atrocity! How much longer will the world be an accomplice ignoring terror? Close the sky right now! Stop the killings! You have power but you seem to be losing humanity."

Regional Governor Pavlo Kyrylenko said Russia had carried out the attack on the hospital during an agreed ceasefire that was meant to allow the evacuation of civilians from the besieged southern city.

President Zelensky's call to "close the sky" was a direct reference to NATO's refusal to introduce a no-fly zone over Ukraine.

He upped the ante after the hospital in southern Ukraine was attacked, demanding again that Western countries declare a no-fly zone over Ukraine.

"Europeans, you can't say you didn't see what happened to Ukrainians. You saw. You know. You have to tighten the sanctions so that Russia no longer has any opportunity to continue this genocide," he said.

By the middle of March President Zelensky was telling the world that 97 children had been killed in Russian attacks.

Another example of Russian obfuscation: President Putin said several times that only professional soldiers had been sent into Ukraine. The Russian defence ministry however acknowledged after three weeks that some conscripts were taking part in the conflict with Ukraine. Conscripts may also have included prisoners.

It was also revealed that troops from Chechnya were involved in the assault on Kyiv. Reuters news agency reported that Ramzan Kadyrov, the leader of Russia's Chechnya region and an ally of President Putin, said he had traveled into Ukraine to meet Chechen troops.

Kadyrov, who has described himself as Putin's "foot soldier," posted videos of heavily armed Chechen troops in the Kyiv region as part of Russia's invasion force.

He has been accused several times by the United States and European Union of rights abuses.

Moscow fought two wars with separatists in Chechnya, a mainly Muslim region in southern Russia, after the 1991 break-up of the Soviet Union.

President Zelensky has been the subject of a smear campaign by Russia for his stout resistance and preference for alliances with the West.

In one broadcast, state-backed Rossiya 1 TV channel identity Dmitry Kiselyov said President Zelensky appeared in an "obscene state" and appeared "under the influence of alcohol or hard drugs" and "insane."

Kiselyov, regarded by some as Putin's "propagandist-in-chief" said in a news program: "Ukraine's Western allies tried their best to convey a simple idea to President Zelensky. No-one will send their troops to Ukraine, no-one will close the airspace over Ukraine, because this will lead to a direct clash between the armies of NATO and Russia.

"It is also better for Ukrainians to forget about joining NATO and the EU.

"Ukraine for the USA and Europe is expendable material; its historical mission is to sh*t on Russia and that's all.

"By the end of the week, Zelensky finally began to understand something. He appeared in such an obscene state that everyone had only one question: Was the head of Ukraine under the influence alcohol or hard drugs? He looked so sluggish and insane."

Moscow TV programs do not refer to "war" or "invasion" but instead to Vladimir Putin's "special military operation" to bring "peace" and root out "Nazis".

According to the state-backed Channel 1 "the service personnel of the Ukrainian army are laying down their weapons and saying that we are one people."

This outlet and Rossiya 1 both claimed the Zelensky government was in its "death throes," suggesting the President had fled Kyiv, ignoring evidence to the contrary.

State-run media also has claimed the Russians only just got to Ukraine in time because Ukraine was "merely a few months away from having a nuclear explosive device."

State TV also aired claims that Ukraine had been involved in bio-warfare research but ahead of the conflict there "all stockpiles and pathogens" were "urgently destroyed."

China also entered the fray with some wild claims about US involvement in Ukraine, the statements reminiscent of the questions that were asked of China about the origins of the Covid pandemic.

A Chinese official accused the US of running biolabs in the eastern Ukraine, claiming the situation was "dangerous" and that the "safety" of the supposed labs was at risk.

"Under the current circumstances, for the sake of the health and safety of people in Ukraine, the surrounding region and the whole world, we call on all relevant parties to ensure the safety of these laboratories," Chinese Foreign Ministry spokesman Zhao Lijian said.

"In particular, the US, as the party with the best knowledge of these laboratories, should release relevant details as soon as possible, including what viruses are stored and what research has been conducted.

"What is the real intention of the US? What exactly did it do?"

The conspiracy theory appears to have originated in Russia in early 2020.

In April that year, the US embassy in Ukraine issued a statement hitting back at the rumors, slamming them as "Russian disinformation regarding the strong US-Ukrainian partnership to reduce biological threats."

It needs to be kept in mind that the bio labs in Ukraine are old ones established in the Soviet era. Ukraine said they were being converted for use as research centers.

The US State Department compiled a Fact v Fiction account of statements made during the conflict.

Some of the fictions espoused by Russia, according to the State Department, include:

- Ukraine and Ukrainian government officials are the aggressor in the Russia-Ukraine relationship.
- The West is pushing Ukraine toward a conflict.
- Russia's deployment of combat forces is a mere repositioning of troops on its own territory.
- Russia is defending ethnic Russians in Ukraine.
- NATO has plotted against Russia since the end of the Cold War, encircled Russia with forces, broken supposed promises not to enlarge, and threatened Russia's security with the prospect of Ukrainian membership in the Alliance.
- The West shuns diplomacy and goes straight to measures like sanctions.

CHAPTER 4
APPEAL TO THE EU PARLIAMENT

Transcript of Ukrainian **President Volodymyr Zelensky**'s *speech to the European Parliament, March 1, 2022.*

This morning was a very tragic one for us. Two cruise missiles hit Kharkiv, the city, which is located to the borders of the Russian federation.

There were always many Russians there and they were always friend, there were warm relations there. More than 20 universities are there. It's the city that has the largest number of universities in our country.

The youth is bright, smart there. The people who gathered there all the time and was gathering there all the time for celebrating all celebrations in the largest square in our country — the Freedom Square. This is the largest square in Europe and that's true.

This is called the Freedom Square. Can you imagine, this morning, two cruise missiles hit this Freedom Square. Dozens killed. This is the price of freedom.

We're fighting just for our land and for our freedom.

Despite the fact that all the cities of our country are now blocked nobody is going to enter and intervene with our freedom and believe you me, every square from today, no matter what it's called, is going to be called Freedom Square, in every city of our country.

Nobody's going to break us, we're strong, we're Ukrainians.

We want our children to live. It seems to me that this is fair. Yesterday, 16 children died. And again, President Putin will say "this is an operation, and we are beating the military infrastructure." Where are our children? What military factories do they work at? ON which rockets? Maybe they ride in tanks? You killed 16 children!

We are fighting for our rights — freedom and life — and now we are fighting for survival. And this is our main motivation. But we are also fighting to be equal members of Europe. The EU will be much stronger with us. Without you, Ukraine will be alone.

Do prove that you are with us. Do prove that you will not let us go. Do prove that you are indeed Europeans, and then life will win over death and light will win over darkness. Glory to Ukraine.

Ruslan Stefanchuk, *Speaker of the Verkhovna Rada of Ukraine. (The following is a transcription of the interpretation of the original speech from Ukrainian into English.)*

First of all, I would like to thank you for giving me the opportunity to address the European Parliament. I would also like to say, look behind me. You see the same shots that the whole world sees today.

Eight years ago, the Ukrainian people categorically said no to Russian aggression, to their attempt to change their eternal path home — to the united European Union and to the very successful process of unification that it has demonstrated over all these years.

Instead, our rights to develop and to be a democratic state that chooses its own path has been completely laid waste by a country that doesn't respect international law or international principles, that disdains territorial integrity and sovereignty. You see the results of that today very clearly in the number of people killed and wounded.

You are aware that the aggressor carried out a full-scale attack on Kharkiv. Today other cities are under constant attack. I believe that this is a crossroads in the history of Europe. Europe is now fighting against an aggressor, and it is very important how the united European community responds to this challenge of savagery and barbarism.

Dear Members, I know you will be looking at a whole range

of serious economic sanctions that you will adopt against the aggressor. I would like you to understand that today Ukraine is defending the border of the civilized world. If, God forbid, Ukraine falls, nobody knows where the Russian aggressor will stop.

When I was in my official suit and we were working in the Verkhovna Rada, we were adopting very important reformist laws, but just today I had to go down to the basement four times, because enemy planes are flying over my one-and-a-half thousand-year-old city, dropping bombs and firing missiles. They are doing everything to break the Ukrainian spirit, but this will not happen.

Think for a moment about what will happen to Europe if the terrible Russian Empire is restored. Would the European Union be able to protect this space of freedom, which it has created over the last dozens of years? What will happen in Eastern European countries now when Russian tanks approach their borders? To what other regions will the Kremlin look after it has conquered Ukraine?

I would like to call upon you to think strategically, to support the unity of the European Union, to support Ukraine, to make it a strategic partner and — most importantly — to act. Don't be silent. Gather all your efforts and show that Europe today is more unified than ever before, because the threat today is greater than ever.

The best support for the people of Ukraine in their darkest hours would be the immediate recognition of our membership of the European Union. Membership of the European Union — even before these events that started on 24 February — was supported by the majority of Ukrainians. Our mandate is to have a relationship with you, with the European Union, because the Ukrainian people have made their choice. I am calling upon all the Member States and the leadership of the European Union to support candidate status for Ukraine, which is now supported by the whole of Ukraine.

You know that Volodymyr Zelensky has already signed a letter with our application for membership, pursuant to Article 49 of the Treaty on European Union.

Dear friends, this motion for a resolution of the European Parliament contains a whole range of sanctions that you plan to impose on the aggressor. I would call on you to support them. Let us together refute Winston Churchill's famous saying that "we live in an era of big events and small people." I know for sure that Ukraine is a great country of great people, and they have proved this over the past six days.

Let us be worthy of those people who are dying right now for the European Union, for the future of our European home. Let us understand that there cannot be peace in Europe without Ukraine. Europe cannot be whole without Ukraine. Glory to Ukraine!

Thank you for your attention.

(The House accorded the Speaker a standing ovation.)

Ursula von der Leyen, *President of the Commission.*

Madam President of the European Parliament, Mr President of the Council, High Representative, Mr President of the Ukraine, dear Volodymyr, Mr Speaker of the Ukrainian Parliament, my honorable Members, war has returned to Europe. Almost 30 years after the Balkan Wars, and over half a century after Soviet troops marched into Prague and Budapest, civil defense sirens again went off in the heart of a European capital. Thousands of people fleeing from bombs camped in underground stations — holding hands, crying silently, trying to cheer each other up. Cars lined up towards Ukrainian Western borders, and when many of them ran out of fuel, people picked up their children and their backpacks and marched for tens of kilometers towards our Union. They sought refuge inside our borders, because their country was not safe any longer. Because inside Ukraine, a gruesome death count has begun. Men, women, children are dying, once again, because a foreign leader, President Putin, decided that their country, Ukraine, has no right to exist. And we will never, ever let that happen and never, ever accept that.

(Applause)

Honorable Members, this is a moment of truth for Europe. Let me quote the editorial of one Ukrainian newspaper, the Kyiv Independent, published just hours before the invasion began: "This is not just about Ukraine. It is a clash of two worlds, two polar sets of values." They are so right. This is a clash between the rule of law and the rule of the gun; between democracies and autocracies; between a rules — based order and a world of naked aggression. How we respond today to what Russia is doing will determine the future of the international system. The destiny of Ukraine is at stake, but our own fate also lies in the balance. We must show the power that lies in our democracies, we must show the power of people that choose their independent paths, freely and democratically. This is our show of force.

Today, a Union of almost half a billion people has mobilized for Ukraine. The people of Europe are demonstrating in front of Russian embassies all across our Union. Many of them have opened their homes to Ukrainians — fleeing from Putin's bombs. And let me thank especially Poland, Romania, Slovakia and Hungary for welcoming these women, men and children. Europe will be there for them, not only in the first days, but also in the weeks and months to come. That must be our promise all together.

(Applause)

This is why we are proposing to activate the temporary protection mechanism to provide them with a secure status and access to schools, medical care and work. They deserve it. We need to do that now. And we know this is only the beginning. More Ukrainians will need our protection and solidarity. We are and we will be there for them.

Our Union is showing a unity of purpose that makes me proud. At the speed of light, the European Union has adopted three waves of heavy sanctions against Russia's financial system, its high — tech industries and its corrupt elite. This is the largest sanctions package in our Union's history. We do not take these measures lightly, but we feel we had to act. These sanctions will take a heavy toll on the Russian economy and on the Kremlin. We are disconnecting key Russian banks from the SWIFT network. We also banned the transactions of Russia's central bank, the single most important financial institution in Russia, and this paralyses billions in foreign reserves, turning off the tap on Russia's and Putin's war. We have to end this financing of his war.

(Applause)

Second, we target important sectors of the Russian economy. We are making it impossible for Russia to upgrade its oil refineries; to repair and modernize its air fleet; and to access many important technologies it needs to build a prosperous future. We have closed our skies to Russian aircraft, including the private jets of oligarchs. And make no mistake: we will freeze their other assets as well — be it yachts or fancy cars or luxury properties — we will freeze that altogether.

Thirdly, in another unprecedented step, we are suspending the licenses of the Kremlin's propaganda machine. The state-owned Russia Today and Sputnik, and all of their subsidiaries, will no longer be able to spread their lies to justify Putin's war and to divide our Union. These are unprecedented actions by the European Union and our partners in response to an unprecedented aggression by Russia.

Each one of these steps has been closely coordinated with our partners and allies, the United States, the United Kingdom, Canada and Norway, but also, for example, Japan, South Korea and Australia. All of these days you see that more than 30 countries — representing well over half of the world's economy — have also announced sanctions and export controls on Russia. If Putin was seeking to divide the European Union, to weaken NATO, and to break the international community, he has achieved exactly the opposite. We are more united than ever and we will stand up in this war, that is clear that we will overcome and we will prevail. We are united and we stay united.

(Applause)

Honorable Members, I am well aware that these sanctions will come at a cost for our economy too. I know this, and I want to speak honestly to the people of Europe. We have endured two years of pandemic. And we all wished that we could focus on our economic and social recovery. But I believe the people of Europe understand very well that we must stand up against this cruel aggression. Yes, protecting our liberty comes at a price. But this is a defining moment. And this is the cost we are willing to pay, because freedom is priceless, honorable Members. This is our principle: freedom is priceless.

Our investments today will make us more independent tomorrow. I 'am thinking first and foremost about our energy security. We simply cannot rely so much on a supplier that explicitly threatens us. This is why we reached out to other global suppliers. And they responded. Norway is stepping up. In January, we had a record supply of LNG gas. We are building new LNG terminals and working on interconnectors. But in the long run, it is our switch to renewables and hydrogen that will make us truly independent. We have to accelerate the green transition. Because every kilowatt-hour of electricity Europe generates from solar, wind, hydropower or biomass reduces our dependency on Russian gas and other energy sources. This is a strategic investment. And, my honorable Members, this is a strategic investment because on top, less dependency on Russian gas and other fossil fuel sources also means less money for the Kremlin's war chest. This is also a truth.

We are resolute, Europe can rise to the challenge. The same is true on defense. European security and defense has evolved more in the last six days than in the last two decades. Most Member States have promised deliveries of military equipment to Ukraine. Germany announced that it will meet the 2% goal of NATO as soon as possible. And our Union, for the first time ever, is using the European budget to purchase and deliver military equipment to a country that is under attack. EUR 500 million from the European Peace Facility, to support Ukraine's defense. As a first batch, we will now also match this by at least EUR 500 million from the EU budget to deal with the humanitarian consequences of this tragic war, both in the country and for the refugees.

Honorable Members, this is a watershed moment for our Union. We cannot take our security and the protection of people for granted. We have to stand up for it. We have to invest in it. We have to carry our fair share of the responsibility.

This crisis is changing Europe. But Russia has also reached a crossroads. The actions of the Kremlin are severely damaging the long-term interests of Russia and its people. More and more Russians understand this as well. They are marching for peace and freedom. And how does the Kremlin respond to this? By arresting thousands of them. But ultimately, the longing for peace and freedom cannot be silenced. There is another Russia besides Putin's tanks. And we extend our hand of friendship to this other Russia. Be assured, they have our support.

(Applause)

Honorable Members, in these days, independent Ukraine is facing its darkest hour. At the same time, the Ukrainian people are holding up the torch of freedom for all of us. They are showing immense courage. They are defending their lives. But they are also fighting for universal values and they are willing to die for them. President Zelensky and the Ukrainian people are a true inspiration. And when we last spoke, he told me again about his people's dream to join our Union.

Today, the European Union and Ukraine are already closer than ever before. There is still a long path ahead. We have to end this war. And we should talk about the next steps. But I am sure: nobody in this hemicycle can doubt that a people that stands up so bravely for our European values belongs in our European family.

And therefore, honorable Members, I say long live Europe. And long live a free and independent Ukraine.

My z vamy. Slava Ukraini.

(Loud and sustained applause)

CHAPTER 5
SANCTIONS

Russia was hit by a wave of sanctions immediately after its invasion of Ukraine began on February 24. As conflict dragged on, more and more sanctions were announced.

Russia hit back, with bans on a string of exports until the end of 2022.

The ban covered telecoms, medical, vehicle, agricultural, and electrical equipment, as well as some forestry products including timber.

Further measures could include restricting access of foreign ships to Russian ports.

Russia's Prime Minister Mikhail Mishustin said the bans would include exports of goods made by foreign companies operating in Russia, such as cars, railway carriages, and containers.

Russia's former president Dmitry Medvedev warned that assets owned by Western companies that pulled out of Russia could be nationalized.

Those reactions should not have been unexpected

Foreign Governments reacted swiftly to Russia's action, imposing sanctions related to finance and trade.

The impact was almost instant — the value of Russia's currency collapsed, a ruble worth less than one US cent. Russia's inflation rate rose more than 2% in the first week of the invasion, the fastest rise since 1998.

The most significant sanctions were moves against Russian oil. The US, UK and EU all announced bans and restrictions on Russian oil imports.

Russia turned to India to shore up its oil exports. According to two Indian officials, reports said, India was considering taking up a Russian offer to buy its crude oil and other commodities at discounted prices with payment via a rupee-ruble transaction.

India and Russia (then the Soviet Union) had a long strategic relationship. During the Cold War the countries also had military, economic and diplomatic relationships.

After the dissolution of the Soviet Union, Russia inherited its close relationship with India, terming their links as a "special and privileged strategic partnership."

Some international traders have been avoiding Russian oil to avoid becoming entangled in sanctions, but the Indian official said sanctions did not prevent India importing the fuel. (India abstained from UN votes condemning the Russian invasion of Ukraine.)

Work was ongoing to set up a rupee-ruble trade mechanism to be used to pay for oil and other goods, the official said.

Sporting organizations also were quick off the blocks to

censure Russia.

Russian and Belarus athletes heading for Beijing for the Winter Olympics in February were turned away by the International Olympic Committee.

FIFA and UEFA announced jointly that they had suspended all Russian international and club teams from their football competitions "until further notice." That ruled Russia out of its World Cup play-off against Poland.

In the UK, the Government imposed sanctions on Roman Abramovich, one of the world's richest men, who was owner of the Chelsea Football Club. UK ministers accused him of having "clear connections" to Vladimir Putin's regime and being among a group of businessmen who had "blood on their hands."

He was one of seven Russians worth up to 15bn pounds whose British assets were frozen and were banned from travelling to Britain.

Abramovich had already put his ownership of Chelsea on the market, but that plan was in limbo by the freezing of his assets.

Foreign secretary Liz Truss also said oligarchs (wealthy Russians with links to President Putin) would "have no place in our economy or society."

"With their close links to Putin, they are complicit in his aggression. The blood of the Ukrainian people is on their hands. They should hang their heads in shame," she said.

Motor racing governing bodies scrubbed competitions

held in both Russia and Belarus and prohibited the use of both countries' flags and anthems, "until further notice." The Haas F1 team terminated the contract of Russian driver Nikita Mazepin and its title sponsor Uralkali.

The World Athletics Council banned all athletes from Russia and Belarus from competing in World Athletics Series events.

The International Tennis Federation (ITF) suspended the Russian Tennis Federation (RTF) and Belarus Tennis Federation (BTF) from ITF membership and from participation in ITF international team competition "until further notice." The ITF also canceled all its competitions scheduled for Russia and Belarus. Russia and Belarus could not compete in the 2022 Davis Cup or 2022 Billie Jean King Cup but players were allowed to compete as individuals on both the ATP and WTA Tours and at grand slams (the ban on Russia saw Australia take up the vacant place in the Davis Cup).

According to CNN, the world governing bodies of a wide range of sports also imposed sanctions on Russian and Belarus competitors, including suspension from competition and competing under national flags. The sports affected were: archery; badminton, baseball and softball, basketball, biathlon, canoeing, chess, curling, cycling, gymnastics, hockey, ice hockey, judo, pentathlon, rowing, rugby, sailing, skating, skiing, surfing, swimming, taekwondo, triathlon and volleyball.

Public pressure then saw businesses that traded in Russia follow suit.

In a move that seemed to stun Russian people more than any other, McDonald's, Coca-Cola and Starbucks suspended their operations in Russia.

"We cannot ignore the needless human suffering unfolding in Ukraine," the fast-food giant McDonald's said, as it announced the temporary closure of all 850 restaurants in Russia, where it employs 62,000 people.

The impact of the announcement in Russia was immediate; massive queues formed outside McDonald's drive-throughs and restaurants.

The list of sanctions grew rapidly. Some entities took longer to act than others but eventually read the "mood of the meeting."

PepsiCo said that despite halting sales in Russia of its flagship beverage, as well as 7Up and Mirinda, it would continue to offer products such as milk and baby food.

"By continuing to operate, we will also continue to support the livelihoods of our 20,000 Russian associates and the 40,000 Russian agricultural workers in our supply chain," PepsiCo CEO Ramon Laguarta said.

Starbucks, which had 130 coffee shops in Russia, said all operations were suspended.

Yum! Brands, whose approximately 1,000 KFC and 50 Pizza Hut restaurants in Russia were almost all independently owned, announced it was closing operations at the company-owned KFC locations.

The company said it was "finalizing an agreement" to do the same with its Pizza Hut restaurants. All profits from operations in Russia would be redirected to "humanitarian efforts."

Heineken joined the exodus of Western brands from Russia; the Dutch brewer said the war was "unprovoked and completely unjustified" and it would stop advertising and selling Heineken beer in Russia. Carlsberg followed suit.

Universal Music Group, the world's biggest label, suspended all operations and closed its offices in Russia.

American movie studios, including Walt Disney Co. and Warner Bros., said they had delayed release of highly anticipated films in Russia.

Netflix Inc. suspended its service that it launched less than a year previously. The company had said earlier it would not comply with a new regulation that required the platform to carry several state-run broadcasters.

IKEA closed its Russian stores, stopped production in the country and stopped all exports and imports to and from Russia and Belarus.

Nike Inc. said it was temporarily closing the stores it owned and operated in Russia,

FedEx Corp. and United Parcel Service Inc. suspended shipments into Russia.

Apple Inc. stopped selling iPhones and other products in Russia.

Russia's RT News and Sputnik News apps were no longer available for download through Apple's App Store outside Russia.

Google suspended all advertising in Russia. The country's communications censor accused YouTube's video service of spreading misinformation and stoking protests.

TikTok suspended new video uploads and live streaming in Russia in response to a new law threatening prison for anyone publishing what authorities considered to be false information about the invasion. (TikTok, known in China as Douyin, is a video-based social network owned by Chinese company ByteDance Ltd.)

The list of companies suspending or withdrawing activity in Russia grew as the invasion stretched on.

American reports said a team from Yale University that monitored companies with a significant presence in Russia listed about 290 that announced withdrawal from the country. This was said to be reminiscent of "the large-scale corporate boycott of apartheid South Africa in the 1980s." About 30 multinationals remained on the list of companies with significant exposure to Russia.

Sanctions were seen as vital in communicating to Russian people what was happening in Ukraine, information they were being denied by State-run media.

Tim Fort, a professor of business ethics at Indiana University, told the AFP news service: "Russians can survive without the Big Mac, but they may ask 'why is McDonald's closed? What's going on?' — it's a more powerful signal in that sense."

The financial and commercial sanctions were sending a message to Russia that it could not do what it was doing in Ukraine and expect to participate in the international economy.

The European Union went further than financial sanctions: a Formula One driver and a Russian previously linked to a £300 million mansion — that is London's second largest house after Buckingham Palace — were among 160 individuals added to an EU sanctions list designed to squeeze Vladimir Putin's "closest circle."

The economic sanctions imposed on Russia with broad consensus among Western governments along with the voluntary withdrawal of multinationals "is really the best way to deal with Russia," according to Richard Painter, a former White House ethics lawyer and a professor at the University of Minnesota.

The food, Beveridge and entertainment companies were joined by some worldwide financial industry brands.

Visa Inc. and Mastercard Inc. suspended their Russian operations. Foreigners wouldn't be able to use their Visa or Mastercard cards for purchases in the country, online or in person. Russian cardholders would still be able to use these cards for purchases in Russia.

American Express Co. also cut off its service in Russia. Globally issued AmEx cards wouldn't work at merchants or ATMs in Russia, and cards issued by Russian banks wouldn't work outside Russia on the AmEx network, the company said.

PayPal Holdings Inc. suspended operations in Russia, including its international money-transfer service Xoom.

The financial card pull-back left many Russians stranded abroad without access to funds.

An extensive range of political identities and wealthy oligarchs and their families were subject to sanctions that included freezing of assets, travel bans and blacklisting of businesses.

The US, UK and EU set about freezing the assets of President Vladimir Putin and his foreign minister, Sergei Lavrov, and banned people and businesses from dealing with the Russian central bank, its finance ministry and its wealth fund.

Some Russian banks were removed from the international financial messaging system Swift that enabled the smooth transfer of money across borders. The ban would delay the payments Russia received for its oil and gas exports.

His foreign-held assets were frozen, but President Putin was still allowed to travel to those jurisdictions. The reason for the asset freeze, according to the EU, was his recognition of the independence of Donetsk and Luhansk, ordering the Russian armed forces into those areas and for the full-scale invasion of Ukraine.

Belarus, accused of aiding Russia's invasion, also faced sanctions from the EU, US and UK.

Other Western allies, including Japan, Canada, Australia and South Korea, also adopted sanctions on Russia.

Russia's first reaction was to more than double its key interest rate to try to stem the decline of the ruble.

Russian authorities, facing potential economic calamity as Western sanctions took hold, threatened foreign companies hoping to withdraw from the country, with arrests and asset seizures, the *Wall Street Journal* reported.

Russian prosecutors issued warnings to several foreign entities (via calls, letters and in-person visits) including to Coca-Cola, McDonald's, Procter & Gamble, IBM and Yum Brands.

Russia also blocked interest payments to foreign investors who held government bonds and banned Russian companies from paying overseas shareholders.

Russia stopped foreign investors who hold tens of billions of dollars of Russian stocks and bonds from selling their assets.

The EU was worried many wealthy Russians would now convert their ruble savings into cryptocurrencies — such as Bitcoin — to bypass the sanctions. Many of the world's largest crypto exchanges refused to impose a blanket ban on Russian clients.

CHAPTER 6
CONSEQUENCES

A humanitarian and refugee crisis to rival that of World War II unfolded as Russia waged war on Ukraine from February 24, 2022.

In just three weeks an estimated 2.5 million Ukrainians had fled their homes, many seeing their safety and future more assured in neighboring countries and Europe.

Domestic civilian flights were canceled on the first day of the invasion and people began heading west and south. For those who escaped, Poland was the most popular destination, so much so that Warsaw said after three weeks that it "was full up."

Romania, Moldova and Hungary also were preferred destinations.

The "safe" corridors supposedly set up by Russia were not so safe at all — mostly they led to Russia and its ally Belarus. At times the corridors came under attack from Russian firepower — ceasefire announcements usually were not backed up by actions.

During a supposed ceasefire on March 9 a Russian air strike severely damaged a children's and maternity hospital in the southern port city of Mariupol, killing and injuring several people.

United Nations High Commissioner for Refugees (UNHCR) figures showed only just more than 1% of those fleeing from Ukraine headed for Russia.

Poland to the west, sharing a 500 km (310 mi) border with Ukraine, proved to be a good friend to Ukraine, also the conduit for supplies, including weaponry from supporting countries, to the besieged President and his people. Poland's supply routes into Ukraine were nominated by Russia as a legitimate target, raising fears of a possible direct attack on a NATO member and prompting warnings from the US about any such action.

Russia, aware of the supply routes, attacked a NATO backed military base in Ukraine near the Poland border on March 13, killing more than 30 people.

(Poland became a North Atlantic Treaty Organisation (NATO) member in 1999 with the Czech Republic and Hungary, the first three countries of the former Soviet bloc and first former members of the Warsaw Pact to join the US-backed defense alliance).

The refugees, mostly women and children (Ukrainian men were not allowed to leave as they were legally obliged to help defend the country) were welcomed in Poland but longed to go home again. Some still had family in Ukraine. Fourteen-year-old Dariy Gulyk hadn't heard from his father for three days and was worried. "In Poland, it's very cool," he told a journalist, "but we want to go home — because home is home."

The UN refugee agency said conditions were bleak in border areas where refugees gathered; temperatures were freezing, and many people spent days on the road waiting to cross.

Polish authorities offered comprehensive help to refugees, including free train travel and access to healthcare. Poland also dropped its requirement to show a negative Covid test.

Hungary opened sections of its border that had been closed to migration. In Moldova, networks of volunteers provided support and hosting families crossing the border.

Germany and Austria offered free train travel.

Meanwhile, the US pledged consequences over the killing of an American journalist in Ukraine who was working on a documentary about refugees.

Filmmaker Brent Renaud, 50, was killed by Russian fire near Irvin, west of Kyiv.

Kyiv region police chief, Andrei Nebitov, said: "The occupiers are cynically killing even journalists of international media who are trying to show the truth about the atrocities of Russian troops in Ukraine."

US national security adviser Jake Sullivan told CNN: "If… an American journalist was killed, it is a shocking and horrifying event. It is one more example of the brutality of Vladimir Putin and his forces as they've targeted schools and mosques and hospitals and journalists.

"And it is why we are working so hard to impose severe

consequences on him, and to try to help the Ukrainians with every form of military assistance we can muster, to be able to push back against the onslaught of these Russian forces."

Just days after Renaud's death, two journalists working for Fox News were killed, according to the US network. Cameraman Pierre Zakrzewski, 55, and Oleksandra Kuvshinova, 24, were killed when their vehicle was hit by incoming fire in Horenka, on the outskirts of Kyiv. A colleague, Benjamin Hall, 39, was wounded.

According to Ukrainian parliament's human rights chief Lyudmyla Denisova at least two Ukrainian journalists had also been killed in the conflict.

Widespread support around the world for President Zelensky by way of aid and sanctions, was reflected in his approval rating at home.

More than 90% of Ukrainians backed their president as Ukraine continued to resist Russia's invasion, according to a national poll conducted by the Ratings Sociological Group.

Polling in March showed the president's approval ratings almost tripled since December 2021, when just 31% of Ukrainians supported him.

There was still a long way to go before there would be any kind of resolution in the Russia-Ukraine conflict.

Russia remained resolute in its demands, even though negotiations were being attempted but not seriously progressed and no common ground established.

Putin appeared to have believed, correctly, the support of NATO, the US and other European governments would not extend to sending troops. Many leaders made reference to starting World War III, preferring instead to impose harsh sanctions.

US President Biden said: "There were two options: start World War III, start a physical war with Russia, or option number two — make a country that acts so contrary to international law pay the price for doing so."

The unanswered question was: "What if Russia assassinated the elected President of a democratic country?" There were reports of up to a dozen attempts on President Zelensky's life.

Russia remained insistent that all its demands be met: Ukraine must surrender and cease military action; change its constitution to enshrine neutrality; not join the NATO bloc; acknowledge Crimea as Russian territory (Russia annexed Crimea — previously conquered by the Russian Empire in 1783 but part of Ukraine since 1991 — in 2014); and recognize the separatist republics of Donetsk and Luhansk as independent states.

From the outset, Ukraine rejected the conditions, drawing support from the West and some neighboring countries.

President Zelensky appeared to soften his stance on some limited points.

"Regarding NATO, I have cooled down regarding this question long ago after we understood that NATO is not prepared to accept Ukraine," the President told American ABC News.

He added: "The alliance is afraid of controversial things and confrontation with Russia. I never wanted to be a country which is begging something on its knees. We are not going to be that country, and I don't want to be that president."

He also said he was open to discussions about the control of Russian-backed separatist regions in eastern Ukraine, which could be an opening for peace talks.

"It is important to me how people who want to be part of Ukraine will live there. I am interested in the opinion of those who see themselves as citizens of the Russian Federation. However, we must discuss this issue," President Zelensky said.

From Russia's perspective any hope President Putin may have had for a speedy victory in Ukraine was dashed; there was no quick surrender.

The Russian army changed its strategy, and began shelling densely populated areas, perhaps signaling a switch to the brutal tactics seen in Grozny during the Chechen war. In 2003 the UN declared Grozny to be the most severely destroyed city in the world.

That was something President Zelensky would not want to see repeated in his country as Russian attacks homed in on the outskirts of Kyiv.

President Zelensky also played down the threat of nuclear attack by Russia that had been mooted because of Russia's expected swift victory not eventuating.

President Putin ordered his nuclear forces on to high alert in response to the wave of sanctions imposed on his country, but President Zelensky dismissed fears Putin would start a nuclear war if the West joined Ukraine's defense.

"I think that the threat of nuclear war is a bluff," President Zelensky told German newspaper *Die Zeit* in a written interview. "It's one thing to be a murderer. It's another to commit suicide. Every use of nuclear weapons means the end for all sides, not just for the person using them. Rather, Putin's threat shows a weakness. You only threaten the use of nuclear weapons when nothing else is working."

But President Zelensky also said the sanctions were not enough to stop Putin.

"If they were, the offensive would have stopped already," he told *Die Zeit*. "Russian oil and gas are still being bought. Western companies still operate on the Russian market while hiding behind various excuses."

The President also sounded the alarm for neighboring countries, including Georgia, Moldova, and the Baltic states, which he said could be next on Russia's target list, a fear shared by some in the West.

Russian Foreign Minister Sergey Lavrov denied Russia posed such a threat.

"We are not planning to attack other countries," Lavrov told a Turkish reporter. "We didn't attack Ukraine either," a demonstrably false statement that would be of little comfort to anyone.

Fears of biological warfare also were raised when Russia alleged the US was operating biowarfare laboratories in Ukraine.

The US and Ukrainian governments have both denied the existence of bioweapons facilities in Ukraine. There are some Ukrainian-run biological threat-analysis and defense labs in Ukraine, but there's no apparent evidence to suggest that they are working on biological weapons as far-right commentators and the Russian government have claimed.

The allegation was seen as a possible false-flag excuse for Russia to use biological weapons. (False-flag operations are when a political or military act is orchestrated in such a way that it appears to have been carried out by a party that is not in fact responsible.)

White House press secretary Jen Psaki tweeted:

We should all be on the lookout for Russia to possibly use chemical or biological weapons in Ukraine, or to create a false flag operation using them.

The use of chemical and biological weapons is banned under the 1925 Geneva protocol. (The Protocol was drawn up and signed at a conference held in Geneva under the auspices of the League of Nations from May 4 to June 17, 1925, and it entered into force on February 8, 1928).

As it was, "conventional warfare was inflicting significant

casualties and many Ukrainians did not escape the Russian bombardment."

The United Nations human rights office said that by March 8 it had verified 1,335 civilian casualties, including 474 killed and 861 injured.

It was noted that the civilian toll was incomplete pending corroboration of reports: "This concerns, for example, the towns of Volnovakha, Mariupol, Izium where there are allegations of hundreds of civilian casualties," the office said.

Ukraine's Ambassador to the UN in Geneva, Yevheniia Filipenko, told the Human Rights council: "Not a day has passed without news of dozens of civilian casualties that resulted from indiscriminate bombing and shelling of residential areas of major Ukrainian cities."

Russia had few direct allies — Belarus was one — but another 35 countries abstained from a United Nations vote condemning the Russian action. Heading those countries were China and India. China's stance was probably not surprising considering it had vowed to return Taiwan to its communist fold, raising fears of military action to do so. China would no doubt hope to learn lessons from the outcome of Russia's action.

China, which had refused to condemn Russia's actions or call them an invasion, repeatedly expressed its opposition to what it described as illegal sanctions on Russia.

It took two weeks for Chinese President Xi Jinping China to

use the "war" word. Speaking at a "virtual meeting" with French President Emmanuel Macron and German Chancellor Olaf Scholz he called for "maximum restraint" in Ukraine and said China was "pained to see the flames of war reignited in Europe." It was his strongest statement thus far on the conflict. He said the three countries (China, France and Germany) should jointly support peace talks between Russia and Ukraine.

A spokesperson for China's Ministry of Foreign Affairs said China "firmly opposed" the sanctions and called them "without any basis" in international law.

"Willfully wielding the stick of sanctions cannot bring peace and security, but will only affect the economy and people's livelihood, lead to a lose-lose situation and aggravate division and confrontation," the spokesperson said, adding that China and Russia had good co-operation and would continue to conduct normal trade relations, including on oil and gas in the spirit of "mutual respect, equality and mutual benefit."

The US warned China against providing military or financial help to Moscow.

According to American officials, Russia had asked for military and economic support from Beijing, which in turn had signaled a willingness to provide aid.

Moscow denied the claim, saying it had enough resources to fulfil its aims. China's foreign ministry labelled the reports on assistance as "disinformation."

State Department spokesperson Ned Price said after

US national security adviser Jake Sullivan met China's top diplomat Yang Jiechi in Rome.

"We will not allow any country to compensate Russia for its losses. We have communicated very clearly to Beijing that we won't stand by."

The sanctions had many consequences for Russia.

Fitch Ratings (a credit ratings agency) downgraded its view of the Russia's government debt, warning a default was "imminent." The ratings cut — from B to C — was the second time in a fortnight Fitch downgraded its view of Russia's ability to pay its debts.

Rival ratings agencies Moody's Investors Service and S&P Global Ratings also slashed their assessments of Russian sovereign debt.

Moscow had already said its bond payments might be affected by sanctions.

Several of Russia's richest businessmen called for peace. One of them, Andrei Melnichenko, known as Russia's coal and fertilizer king, said the war in Ukraine was a tragedy that must be stopped or there would be a global food crisis.

Fertilizer prices worldwide already were too high for many farmers, he said.

"The events in Ukraine are truly tragic. We urgently need peace," Melnichenko, 50, who is Russian but was born in Belarus and has a Ukrainian mother, told Reuters in a statement emailed by his spokesperson.

"As a Russian by nationality, a Belarusian by birth, and a Ukrainian by blood, I feel great pain and disbelief witnessing brotherly peoples fighting and dying."

Melnichenko founded Uralchem, Russia's largest ammonium nitrate producer which is based in Zug, Switzerland, and SUEK, Russia's top coal producer.

"It has already led to soaring prices in fertilizers which are no longer affordable to farmers," he said.

Melnichenko said a supply chain already disrupted by Covid was now even more distressed: "Now it will lead to even higher food inflation in Europe and likely food shortages in the world's poorest countries."

The effects of sanctions and embargoes were not just felt by Russia. The rest of the world saw an almost immediate rise in the cost of oil. The fallout grew daily as countries sympathetic to Ukraine and companies that did business with Russia fell into line with actions designed to support Ukraine and promote disquiet within Russia itself.

Russia was the target of protests around the world, even within Russia, a sign that President Putin might not enjoy the populist support he hoped for.

A new censorship law in Russia threatened prison for anyone calling his invasion a "war" rather than a "special military operation."

Despite such legislation, social media remained active with alternative viewpoints to that of state-controlled media. Troy

Hunt, a cybersecurity specialist based in Australia told Israeli media: "It's never going to be like what it was in the Cold War, in terms of being able to chop off information coming from the West. Obviously it has a big impact. But you've got so many people who have access to technology that can easily circumvent these controls."

President Zelensky has more than 5.1 million followers on Twitter, so his message had far greater reach than perhaps Russia understood.

President Zelensky used speeches and tweets to call for greater action from the West, including a total embargo on Russian oil. Such action was not included in a raft of initial sanctions imposed on Russia, but soon gained traction.

In a plea for greater military help — including planes and a no-fly zone in the region — President Zelensky told US senators, "Don't allow brave and strong people who share your values to be exterminated."

Calls for a no-fly zone remained contentious. President Putin said such an action would constitute a declaration of war, putting NATO and the West on notice.

President Zelensky continued to lambast the West for not taking action and his call for an oil embargo got a positive response days after the first time he addressed more than 300 members of the US Congress.

The meeting, via Zoom, was the first time President Zelensky had addressed both houses of Congress since the invasion. He was to continue to contact with foreign governments over several weeks, reporting on the horrors being inflicted on his people and pleading for support. A second address to Congress a week later elicited a further aid response from the US.

President Biden said in a White House announcement on March 8: "I'm announcing the United States is targeting the main artery of Russia's economy. We're banning all imports of Russian oil and gas and energy. That means Russian oil will no longer be acceptable at US ports and the American people will deal another powerful blow to Putin's war machine."

Europe, much more dependent on Russian oil than the US, had until then remained hesitant to take such action.

But almost simultaneously with the Biden announcement, the UK said it would phase out imports of Russian oil by the end of 2022, the timing deigned to allow negotiation of replacement supply.

On March 16, President Biden signed off on an extra $US 800 million military aid package for Ukraine. The previous day, the US President signed a bill to give $US 13.6 billion for emergency aid to Ukraine.

The EU also announced plans to phase out its reliance on Russia for energy needs "as soon as possible."

At last, the West was heeding Zelensky's pleas.

The Ukrainian President had another problem. His military hardware was no match for the might of the Russian war machine.

Back in December 2021, as the country marked its national army day with a display of US armored vehicles and patrol boats, President Zelensky said his armed forces could fight off any Russian attack.

"The servicemen of the Armed Forces of Ukraine continue to fulfil their most important mission — to defend the freedom and sovereignty of the state from the Russian aggressor," he said.

Two months later, he pleaded for more fighter planes.

The most likely supplier, the US, was not willing to send fighter planes into the conflict for fear of creating a wider war with Russia.

In a surprise move, Poland offered to provide its 28 MiG-29 fighter jets for use by Ukraine. The Pentagon rejected the plan.

The US had been looking at a proposal under which Poland would supply Ukraine with the Mig-29s and in turn receive American F-16s to make up for their loss. Ukrainian pilots were trained to fly the Soviet-era fighter jets.

President Zelensky's plea for military aid did not fall on completely deaf ears.

President Biden ordered the US State Department to release up to an extra $US 350 million worth of weapons from US stocks to Ukraine. That was on top of the $US 1 billion in security assistance to Ukraine over the previous 12 months.

For the first time in its history, the EU financed the

purchase and delivery of arms after leaders agreed to send weapons worth €450 million ($US 502 million) to Kyiv. Some countries had agreed to provide fighter jets, but details were not given.

The UK decided in January to supply Ukraine with "light anti-armor defensive weapon systems." The aid was upgraded in February to include "lethal aid in the form of defensive weapons and non-lethal aid," Prime Minister Boris Johnson announced.

News agencies reported that a wide range of more help was on the way to Ukraine:

France agreed to send more military equipment as well as fuel. It had already acceded to earlier Ukrainian requests for defensive anti-aircraft and digital weapons.

The Netherlands agreed to supply air defense rockets and anti-tank systems and was considering sending a Patriot air defense system, in conjunction with Germany, to a NATO battle group in Slovakia, it said.

Germany pledged 1,000 anti-tank weapons and 500 Stinger surface-to-air missiles, a major shift from Berlin's longstanding policy of banning weapons exports to a conflict zone.

Canada sent lethal military weaponry and agreed to lend Kyiv half a billion Canadian dollars ($US 394 million) for self-defense.

Even non-aligned Sweden contributed to the supply chain to Ukraine, sending 5,000 anti-tank weapons to Ukraine, with

Denmark contributing a further 2,700. Norway sent helmets and body armor and up to 2,000 M72 anti-tank weapons.

Finland, also neutral, agreed to supply weapons: 1,500 rocket launchers, 2,500 assault rifles, 150,000 rounds of ammunition, and 70,000 servings of field rations.

Belgium said it would supply Ukraine with 3,000 more automatic rifles and 200 anti-tank weapons, as well as 3,800 tons of fuel.

Portugal provided night-vision goggles, bulletproof vests, helmets, grenades, ammunition and automatic G3 rifles.

Greece offered "defense equipment" and humanitarian aid.

Romania — which shares a border with Ukraine — offered to treat wounded people in its 11 military hospitals as well as sending fuel, bulletproof vests, helmets and other "military material" worth $US3.3 million.

Spain offered 1,370 grenade launchers, 700,000 rounds of munitions and light automatic weapons.

The Czech Republic said it would provide 4,000 mortars, an arsenal of 30,000 pistols, 7,000 assault rifles, 3,000 machine guns, many sniper rifles and a million bullets.

Croatia provided €16 million of small arms and body armor.

All this aid was seen as ringing endorsement for President Zelensky's vow to his people: "We are defending our independence, our state, and it will remain so."

Unless Russia opted for a short sharp "scorched earth"

campaign, the war was going to be a long haul for both countries.

What was the end game?

The best hope for the people of Ukraine would be a negotiated settlement, but what would their President have to concede?

Certainly he wanted to avoid what happened in the Donbas region of eastern Ukraine where President Putin had already recognized two separatist territories as independent states, ordering the deployment of Russian troops in defiance of international law.

For almost eight years the breakaway enclaves were the site of a low-intensity war between Russian-backed separatists and Ukrainian forces that left more than 14,000 people dead.

The Russian annexation of Crimea (Ukrainian territory) in 2014 also served as a reminder of what could happen.

About 4.20 a.m. at the end of February in 2014, 120 people in full combat gear and automatic weapons took over the buildings of the Parliament and the Council of Ministers of the Autonomous Republic of Crimea. They looked like soldiers, but they did not have any insignia on their uniforms.

They were the first of the so-called "little green men" who appeared on the streets of the capital. Russian flags were hung and barricades were built in front of the doors of the Council of Ministers of the Autonomous Republic of Crimea. It looked like a special forces operation. Later, these events were referred to as "the Moscow landing." The same people appeared in Donbas two months later.

Against that background, it was clear President Putin was not going to withdraw without making some sort of gain.

He appeared to be chasing a bigger prize this time, the rest of Ukraine.

But this time, such was the devastation being inflicted by his soldiers on a neighbor that the Russian people, once the truth became obvious, might even hold the answer by ousting Putin, one way or another.

That would take a popular uprising from within Russia or some other incentive.

A remote possibility was that someone would take the $US 1 million bounty offered by a former Russian businessman for the arrest of Putin. The offer was made by Alex Konanykhin, who left Russia in 1992 and seven years later became the first Russian citizen to be granted political asylum in the United States from post-Soviet Russia.

World War III was an option no one wanted. Not even Russia.

CHAPTER 7

ZELENSKY: BOY, MAN, HUSBAND, ACTOR, PRESIDENT

Vladimir Putin's assertion the invasion (although he never called it that, referring to it as a "special military operation") of Ukraine was about de-Nazifying the country just didn't stack up, even if the cocooned Russian public believed the repeated spin that Ukraine was controlled by a cabal of fascists.

More credible was the view that Putin did not want a close neighbor bringing the West-backed North Atlantic Treaty Organization (NATO) to its doorstep. President Zelensky preferred to align with Europe, not Russia and its allies, and applied for NATO membership.

Allied to that was Putin's view that parts of Ukraine were Russian and should be part of Russia.

The Nazism claims seemed to strike a chord with Russians who had been reminded by Putin of the Soviet Union's role in putting down Nazi aggression in World War II, when millions of Jews were put to death. It was also repeated abroad by

Russian diplomatic missions, including Russia's embassy in South Africa.

South Africa was among 17 African nations to abstain from voting on a UN General Assembly resolution calling for Russia to withdraw from Ukraine.

The Russian embassy in Pretoria claimed on its Twitter account to have "received a great number of letters of solidarity from South Africans, both individuals and organisations... we appreciate your support and glad you decided to stand with us today, when Russia, like 80 years ago, is fighting Nazism in Ukraine."

The embassy's claims reflected those made by Putin when he announced his "special military operation" on February 24, 2022.

Putin insisted his aims were to "demilitarize and de-nazify" Ukraine — a reference to narratives the Kremlin had long propagated in its bid to de-legitimize the Kyiv leadership — in order to "protect" Russian-speakers "subjected to bullying and genocide" in the Donbas.

Germany's chancellor Olaf Scholz branded Mr Putin's claims of a genocide in eastern Ukraine "ridiculous."

Like most countries, Ukraine had its extremists, and they would include neo-Nazis. But could President Volodymyr Zelensky be a Nazi sympathizer or be manipulated by them?

Volodymyr Zelensky's life story means the answer would be no.

To begin with, he is Jewish, the first Jew to lead his country. He lost family members during the Holocaust. The Ukrainian Prime Minister, Denys Shmyhal also is Jewish.

The Ukraine government in February 2022 enacted legislation criminalizing antisemitism, in response to a rise in antisemitic vandalism and far-right violence.

Who is Volodymyr Zelensky?

Volodymyr Oleksandrovych Zelensky was born to Jewish parents on January 25, 1978 in the industrial center of Kryvyy Rih, southern Ukraine, then part of the Union of Soviet Socialist Republics.

His father, Oleksandr Zelensky, was a professor and the head of the Department of Cybernetics and Computing Hardware at the Kryvyi Rih State University of Economics and Technology; his mother, Rymma Zelenska, was an engineer. His grandfather, Semyon (Simon) Ivanovych Zelensky, served in the Red Army (in the 57th Guards Motor Rifle Division) during World War II; Semyon's father and three brothers were murdered in the Holocaust.

When a child, Volodymyr's family relocated to Erdenet, Mongolia, for four years before returning to Kryvyy Rih, where he began school.

As did many people from Ukraine's Dnipropetrovsk region, he grew up as a native Russian speaker. But he also became fluent in Ukrainian and aged 16 passed the Test of English as a

Foreign Language. He received an education grant to study in Israel, but his father did not let him to go.

In 1995 he began studies at Kryvyy Rih Economic Institute, a campus of Kyiv National Economic University. He graduated with a law degree and that's where his career appeared to be heading.

But he was also attracted to theatre, forming a group of performers in 1977. They were known as Kvartal 95 ("Quarter 95," the neighborhood in central Kryvyy Rih where he spent his childhood) and appeared in the televised finals of KVN ("Club of the Funny and Inventive People"), an improvisational comedy competition televised throughout the Commonwealth of Independent States (CIS).

Zelensky and Kvartal 95 became regulars on *KVN* until 2003 when he co-founded Studio Kvartal 95, a production company that became one of Ukraine's most successful entertainment studios.

In September 2003 he also married Olena Kiyashko. The pair met at university where she studied architecture and creative writing.

A daughter, Oleksandar, was born in July 2004. She, too, has a taste for acting and appeared in the 2014 movie *8 New Dates* in which she played the protagonist's daughter, Sasha.

In 2016, Oleksandra won 50,000 hryvnias (about $US 1,600) in a show called *The Comedy Comedy's Kids*.

In 2006 Zelensky appeared on the Russian version of *Dancing with the Stars*. He won. He also voiced Paddington

Bear in the Ukrainian release of the animated film.

The Zelenskys' second child, a son named Cyril, was born in January 2013.

Volodymyr Zelensky was artistic director of Kvartal 95 until 2011, when he was appointed general producer of the Ukrainian television channel Inter TV.

He left Inter TV in 2012, and in October that year he and Kvartal 95 signed a joint production agreement with the Ukrainian network 1+1.

The network owner was Ihor Kolomoisky, one of the wealthiest people in Ukraine.

The relationship between Zelensky and Kolomoisky came under scrutiny when Zelensky announced his entry into politics. Was Zelensky a puppet of the rich?

As well as television, Zelensky appeared in feature films, including the historical farce *Rzhevskiy Versus Napoleon* (2012) and the romantic comedies *8 First Dates* (2012) and *8 New Dates* (2015).

In 2013 Zelensky returned to Kvartal 95 as artistic director. But Ukrainian politics was about to go through an upheaval.

In February 2014 President Viktor Yanukovych's government fell after months of mass protests. In May billionaire Petro Poroshenko was elected president.

It was during this period of apparent instability that Russia made its first serious move towards Ukraine.

With a Russian-backed insurgency raging in eastern

Ukraine and corruption undermining public confidence in government, Poroshenko struggled to enact even the most straightforward reforms.

Zelensky, obviously influenced by these events, launched a show called *Servant of the People* on 1+1 in October 2015. His wife, Olena, was a writer on the episodes.

Zelensky cast himself as Vasiliy Goloborodko, a history teacher who became a viral Internet phenomenon after a student filmed him delivering an impassioned and profanity-laden address against official corruption.

The show was a huge hit. Goloborodko's unlikely path to the presidency of Ukraine in the show was later seen as a blueprint for Zelensky's entry into politics. In 2018 Kvartal 95 officially registered "Servant of the People" as a political party in Ukraine.

The 2019 presidential election saw a field of more than three dozen candidates. Zelensky, from the Servant of the People, was one.

On March 31, 2019, Zelensky won more than 30% of the vote in the first round of the presidential election. Incumbent Poroshenko had 16%.

Zelensky did not debate Poroshenko until two days before the second round of polling started. On April 19, 2019, tens of thousands gathered at Kyiv's Olympic Stadium to see the confrontation and, although Poroshenko attempted to portray Zelensky as a political novice who lacked the fortitude to confront Russian President Vladimir Putin, he failed to make any inroads into voter sentiment. A second debate the next day did not go ahead.

On April 21, Zelensky was elected president in a landslide, with 73% of the vote. He was sworn in on May 20, 2019. Life had imitated art.

Four years before, he was one of Ukraine's most popular TV comedians, starring in a satirical TV show and performing in a troupe where he and another man appeared to play a piano with their genitals for five minutes (the full view was obscured).

Video of that performance went viral on YouTube, as did episodes of *Servant of the People*, which was belatedly picked up by various TV networks, including Channel 4 in the UK.

Aged 44, Volodymyr Zelensky was President, his country firmly in the sights of Russian aggressors.

Ukraine election 2019

Population: **43.9m**

GDP per capita: **$US 8,800**

GDP growth: **2.5%**

Ethnic Ukrainians (est): **78%**

Ethnic Russians (est.): **17%**

Unemployment (est.): **9.2%**

Voter turnout 2029: **62.09%**

Vote: **Zelensky 73.22 %, Prooshenko 24.45 %**

Source: BBC and CIA World Factbook

Political parties in Ukraine fall into two major movements — the pro-Western, pro-European, anti-Russian group, of which Zelensky's Servant of the People is the predominant. Others in this group include European Solidarity, Golos (Voice), Radical Party, Strength and Honor and six others, the Ukrainian Democratic Alliance for Reform (UDAR) among them.

UDAR's leader, Ukraine's retired professional heavyweight boxer Vitali Klitschko, is perhaps the most familiar of these in the West, often appearing in TV news reports.

Opposing these parties are the half dozen pro-Russian parties, such as Opposition Platform — For Life and Our Land.

Ideology is not the main driver of these parties, and they all represent a variety of ideologies.

Of the 450 seats in Parliament, 254 are held by Servant of the People, with 25 seats held by the pro-Western European Solidarity and 26 by also pro-Western Batkivshchyna (Fatherland) party. The pro-Russian Opposition Platform holds 43.

Despite the number of candidates, the 2019 presidential election boiled down to a contest between the comedian and the incumbent tycoon — Zelensky and Poroshenko.

Poroshenko pledged to resist Russian aggression. He said the election was no less important than that of 2014, which followed the ousting of a pro-Russian administration.

After the election, Zelensky was the one who faced the

Russian might.

Zelensky was favorite to win in the opinion polls as the final round of voting approached — he had dominated the first round of voting three weeks previously when 39 candidates were on the ballot.

Poroshenko, a billionaire who made his fortune mainly through his confectionery and TV businesses, was elected in 2014 after an uprising overthrew the previous pro-Russian government.

Before the polls opened, there was a court challenge; a man had claimed the distribution of free tickets for a presidential debate by Volodymyr Zelensky's supporters amounted to bribery and called on the court to bar Zelensky from standing. The challenge was rejected.

Zelensky mainly used social media to communicate with the voting public.

He shunned official rallies or political speeches but put out lots of cheerful videos on social media.

He had no previous political experience (apart from his acting role) and his campaign focused on his difference to others rather than on any concrete policy ideas.

"No promises, no disappointment" was one of his statements.

Poroshenko had a more established network on the ground and the support of administrators across the country.

Yet, Zelensky won the first round with more than 30% of

the vote — almost double that of Poroshenko.

Pre-poll surveys showed Ukrainians were seriously dissatisfied with politicians who were widely regarded as corrupt and in the pockets of oligarchs — very rich business leaders with great political influence.

The choice for voters was whether to stick to what they'd had for the past five years in Poroshenko or take a leap into the unknown with Zelenksy, who had not espoused any significant policies other than to clean-up Ukrainian politics by promising to stamp out corruption and loosen the grip of the oligarchs.

The latter pledge raised a few eyebrows as he was backed by billionaire Ihor Kolomoisky, possibly Ukraine's most controversial oligarch.

All Zelensky's TV shows aired on one of Ukraine's most popular TV channels 1+1, owned by Kolomoisky. At the time of the election, Klomoisky was in self-imposed exile in Israel while several investigations into his business dealings were under way in Ukraine.

The President

Volodymyr Zelensky was sworn in as the sixth president of Ukraine on May 20, 2019.

In his inauguration speech, the new President said his then six-year-old son had asked if the announcement that "Zelensky is president" meant that he was too. Although he dismissed it as a child's joke at first, Zelensky said he later understood it as the truth.

"Because every one of us is the president now," he said.

"It's not mine, it's our common victory, and it's our common chance for which we take shared responsibility. And now it wasn't just me who took the oath. Each of us put a hand on the constitution and each of us swore loyalty to Ukraine.

"Imagine screaming headlines: 'President doesn't pay taxes', 'President drunk rushed through red lights', 'President steals a little'. But everybody does the same. You sure agree it is a shame, and that is what I mean when I say that every one of us is the president.

"Starting today, every one of us bears responsibility for Ukraine which we will leave to our children. Each of us, in our places, can do something for the development of Ukraine. A European country starts with everyone. Yes, we have chosen a (political) direction to Europe, but Europe is not somewhere there, Europe is here (pointing to his head). And when Europe is here, it will come to our country. It will be in Ukraine.

"This is our shared dream, but we have shared pains. Each of us died in the Donbas. Every day we lose one of us, and each of us is internally displaced. Those who lost their own homes and those who in turn, opened the doors of their homes, sharing this pain. And each of us is a migrant worker. Those who didn't manage to find their place at home but found earnings in a foreign country. Those who, fighting poverty, had to lose their dignity. But we will overcome all of this, for each of us is a Ukrainian.

"We are all Ukrainians. There's no less of a Ukrainian or more of a Ukrainian, the right Ukrainian or wrong Ukrainian, we are all Ukrainians. From Uzhhhorod to Luhansk, from Chernihiv to Simferopol, in Lviv, Kharkiv, in Donetsk, Dnipro, and Odessa — we are all Ukrainians."

Within days, President Zelensky faced his first foreign policy challenge when Russia's President Putin announced he would offer Russian passports to the Ukrainian citizens in separatist-controlled areas of war-torn eastern Ukraine.

The Russian-backed conflict there was five years old and hundreds of thousands of Ukrainians had been displaced.

Zelensky ridiculed the offer and responded on social platform Facebook that he would extend Ukrainian citizenship to Russians and others "who suffer from authoritarian or corrupt regimes."

His next task was to dissolve the Verkhovna Rada (Ukraine Supreme Council), necessary as his personal victory did not come with a legislative mandate as Servant of the People did not hold any seats in parliament.

Snap elections were held on July 21, Zelensky saying the contest was "maybe more important than the presidential election."

Servant of the People won an absolute majority — 254 of 450 seats (26 seats, representing Crimea — a Ukrainian

autonomous republic that was annexed by Russia in 2014 —
and the war zone in the east, were not contested).

It was the first time in Ukraine's post-Soviet history that a
single party commanded absolute control over the legislative
process.

Ties to President Zelensky's former business partner again
were scrutinized. Kolomoisky's media empire provided a
platform for Zelensky during the presidential campaign, but
Zelensky vowed that no special favors would be granted.

Kolomoisky had returned to Ukraine just before the
inauguration; the billionaire giving an assurance he would not
act as a "grey cardinal," directing policy from off-stage.

Polling by the Ratings Sociological Group showed that by
December 2021, just 31% of Ukrainians approved of President
Zelensky.

By March 2022, two weeks after the Russian invasion began,
Zelensky's approval rating almost tripled to more than 90%.

In the lead-up to the December 2019 opinion poll, there
were doubts whether the 44-year-old had the political nous to
lead the country during an existential crisis.

That changed just before the Russian invasion began in
February 2022, when the man who had been a comedian put
on a serious face of a wartime leader to tell Russia: "When you
attack us you will see our faces, not our backs, but our faces."

It was the first real indication that Russia would be
confronted by a Ukrainian leader who was not going to be a

"pushover" and who had massive support at home and abroad.

According to *Newsweek* magazine, quoting the President's office, the leader survived around a dozen assassination attempts in the first two weeks of the Russian invasion.

Mikhail Podolyak, head of the office for the President, said international reports that three attempts have been made against Zelensky's life were false. He said: "Our foreign partners are talking about two or three attempts. I believe that there were more than a dozen such attempts."

President Zelensky rejected the notion by some media commentators that he was similar to King Leonidas of the Spartans, who faced down the Persians at the Battle of Thermopylae in 480 BC.

"I don't want Ukraine's history to be a legend about 300 Spartans. I want peace," he declared, adding that he didn't even want to lose the battle in order to eventually win the war — as the Spartans did. "We are on our land. We are ready for anything."

The First Lady

When her husband first expressed an interest in real-life politics, Olena was "aggressively opposed" to the idea, reports said. She admitted she was skeptical.

"When I was told that it would happen, I was already prepared to have little changes in my and family life. I can spoil the mood, do not support, put obstacles, but it's not constructive… I try to keep myself, calm down. So far, it seems that I can do it," she said in an interview with *Opinionua.com*.

She described herself as primarily supporting her husband: "So far, I've taken time out in order not to think about it. I know this is a difficult role… In general, the First Lady does not have to take any main roles. This tandem should repeat what is happening in the family. We have the leader and I try to support him. When someone takes responsibility — it's very convenient, so I try not to drag too much attention to myself."

In an interview with the magazine *Vogue Ukraine*, she said: "I am a non-public person. But the new realities [being First Lady] require their own rules, and I'm trying to comply with them."

Olena first found out about her husband's candidacy on social media. She told *Vogue* she said to him: "Why didn't you tell me?" His response: "I forgot."

Olena was with her husband during his electioneering.

With her husband winning the presidency, Olena became one of Ukraine's most influential people, and in December 2019 she took part in Ukraine's entry to the G7 international initiative on gender equality, the Biarritz Partnership.

She told *Vogue*: "Life hasn't changed, but circumstances have. I do not have enough time alone with myself. I have got two kids, so I have rarely been alone before. I probably have had my only private space in the car, while driving.

"Now they have deprived me of this — I am always guarded.

Now a bathroom is my only retreat. But I am lucky with people who are in my personal space now: they keep silence when I need this silence and can maintain a conversation when they feel that it's necessary."

Despite her comments about staying calm, Olena Zelenska has been most forthright in speaking out about Russian aggression.

On March 6, 2022, she shared photos on Instagram of five children who died during Russia's attacks.

"I appeal to all the unbiased media in the world! Tell this terrible truth: Russian invaders are killing Ukrainian children," she wrote.

"Tell it to Russian mothers — let them know what exactly their sons are doing here, in Ukraine. Show these photos to Russian women — your husbands, brothers, compatriots are killing Ukrainian children! Let them know that they are personally responsible for the death of every Ukrainian child because they gave their tacit consent to these crimes."

She shared multiple posts in different languages, sharing photos of children. Her post: "The Russian occupiers are killing Ukrainian children. Consciously and cynically.

"18-month-old Kirill from Mariupol was urgently taken to the hospital by his parents. He was wounded by the shelling, and doctors could do nothing.

"Alice from Okhtyrka. She could have turned eight years old. However, she died in the shelling with her grandfather, who was protecting her.

"Polina from Kyiv. She died during the shelling on the streets of our capital, along with her parents and brother. Her sister is in critical condition.

"Arseniy, 14 years old. A fragment of the projectile hit his head. The medics could not reach the boy under the gunfire. Arseniy bled to death.

"Sofia, six years old. She, along with her one-and-half-month-old brother, mother, grandmother and grandfather, were shot to death in their car. The family tried to leave Nova Kakhovka.

"I have to tell you about it. At least 38 children have already died in Ukraine. And this figure might be increasing this very moment due to the shelling of our peaceful cities!

"When people in Russia say that their troops are not hurting the civilian population, show them these pictures! Show them the faces of these children who weren't even given a chance to grow up. How many more children must die to convince Russian troops to stop firing and allow humanitarian corridors?

"We need corridors in the hottest cities in Ukraine right now! Hundreds of children die there in basements without food and medical care. Russian soldiers shoot families who try to leave the buildings. They also kill volunteers who try to help.

"I appeal to all the unbiased media in the world!

"To NATO countries: close the sky over Ukraine! Save our children, because tomorrow it will save yours! #NoFlyZoneUA #closeUAskyNOW #NATOclosethesky #stoprussia."

Olena Zalenska has been in contact with other First Ladies around the world. Another post: "The First Ladies are asking me these days how they can help Ukraine. My answer is — tell the truth to the world!" she wrote. "Speak up! What is happening in Ukraine is not a 'special military operation,' as Putin says, but a full-scale war, where the aggressor is the Russian Federation."

CHAPTER 8

SERVANT OF THE PEOPLE: THE TV SHOW

The birth of Zelensky as a political figure is accepted as his role in *Servant of the People*, a TV satire series on politics in Ukraine. But in this August 22, 2017 interview with Anthony Kao of *Cinema Escapist*, Zelensky reveals much of the real birth of what became his political persona.

Q: From what I've read, you have a very interesting life story. You spent part of your childhood in Mongolia, had aspirations of being a diplomat before deciding to instead study law at one of Ukraine's top universities… and now you're one of Ukraine's most popular actors. How'd that happen?

A: Everything was rather spontaneous. [Narrating in the second person…] You never know where you'll be tomorrow. You go to school, then your parents move to work in Mongolia and you obviously have to go with them. You turn eighteen and want to study international relations to be a diploma —

but you're told it's expensive, it's hard to do, and you need to move to the capital (for the USSR, Moscow).

Instead, you go to law school and start taking part in a local theater club, and then you start doing games with the university KVN (a popular Russophone comedy franchise) team. That later progresses to a higher level: the official KVN comedy show on TV (for Americans, think of a Russian *Saturday Night Live*).

Throughout this process, you have to gradually say goodbye to some of your dreams. Sometimes you think you totally control the situation, but in reality, it's like you're guided in some way, as if destiny is building your career in a way that you didn't intend.

Q: How did you and others at Kvartal 95 (the production studio Zelensky helms) first come up with the idea of *Servant of the People*?
A: We first came up with the idea sometime in the early 2000s. Back then, the political situation in Ukraine wasn't so challenging. Despite the fact that people weren't very interested in politics at the time, we still somehow fantasized about and came up with the idea of a commoner becoming the head of state.

The initial idea was a bit different [from today's *Servant of the People*] though. We first thought it would be some kind of reality TV show, where ordinary people would come on as candidates and other people would vote for them. Maybe someday we'll return to that original idea, but we decided to do a traditional series format because that became more popular.

Q: Why do you think *Servant of the People* has become so popular amongst Ukrainians?

A: Well, first, it touches upon a universal desire: all normal people want to live a better life. As the expression goes, a fish rots from the head down. Therefore, everyone wants decent people at top. When you have that, everyday life can be more normal, and then you don't have to think about survival on a daily basis. When that happens, you can think of other issues, more global ones — like the environment and so on.

Additionally — our corruption problems stem from the Soviet era, and the people in power today are mostly from that generation. Ukrainians who want positive changes can see a bit of themselves in our show's characters [who represent a change from the old order]. If a teacher can become President in our TV series, maybe a great surgeon can someday become a Minister of Health, or a cool IT specialist turns into the head of the information security department. Admittedly real life might not be so simple, but *Servant of the People* isn't exactly simple either.

That brings me to another point: our show's genre is very multifaceted and quite new for Ukrainian TV. It's not just a comedy, it's a political comedy with hints of satire and drama. Ultimately, it's very up-to-date and reflects the current sentiments of people. I think that makes it popular.

Q: How has the success of *Servant of the People* affected your personal life? Do you get a lot more people wanting to take selfies with the "People's President" these days?

A: Yes, people often want to take selfies with me — but not necessarily me as a person. Oftentimes they're looking to take that selfie with [President Goloborodko] the character they see on screen.

Also, Kvartal 95 and I have started receiving more messages from ordinary people that confirm there's a desire for [someone like President Goloborodko] to lead Ukraine through its current realities.

Q: Has playing the President of Ukraine on TV, and creating this show, affected your view about politics at all?

A: While working on this project, we obviously had to research deeper into political topics, which is quite normal for screenwriters, producers, and actors who don't have prior expertise in an area. The deeper we got, the more politically educated we became — but I don't know whether that's for better or for worse.

I will say that some things started looking more like a nightmare, and that compelled me to be more curious about "why" they had to be that way.

Q: Has there been any reaction from Ukraine's oligarchs (which *Servant of the People* lampoons), or President Petro Poroshenko himself, about the show?

A: I haven't heard any direct reactions from them, I just know that people generally like the show.

Although the series is a reflection of today's life, it's also a parallel reality. [Poroshenko] is not a former teacher, and the show's oligarchs are rather generalized characters. Therefore, I don't think that [President Poroshenko and the oligarchs] would be able to project the show's events onto themselves.

Ultimately, *Servant of the People*'s story is very unusual. We didn't intend for it to be moralizing, but I recognize that people might still draw their own inferences.

Q: How has Ukraine's media environment changed — or not changed — since the 2014 Euromaidan Revolution? Do you think that you could've made *Servant of the People* before 2014?

A: Yes, I think we could have. In my opinion, Ukraine's media environment started changing around the time of the first Maidan, the 2004 Orange Revolution. Political humor appeared in our main comedy show *Vecherniy Kvartal* ("Evening Kvartal") around then.

Q: What role do you think satire plays in Ukraine's current political and social landscape?

A: Well satire in general has a long history: you can see it start with Aesop, you can see it with Shakespeare. Of course, satire differs depending on the historical period, current events, and socio-economic context. I'd cite Bulgakov [who was born in Kyiv] as a great satirist who described the realities of his society.

I see satire as a form that you can fill with different content — you can satirize politics, you can satirize love. However, the excellence of language — how sharp, up-to-date, and daring it is, ultimately distinguishes good satire from mediocre satire.

Back to Ukraine — I think satire has been a forte of ours [Kvartal 95] since the early 2000s. We use it in many of our programs, and it's been very popular amongst Ukrainians. And maybe that's due to the fact that contemporary Ukraine has to deal with many challenging and complex political, economic, and social realities.

Q: What differences — or similarities — do you see between post-Soviet humor and American/Western humor?

A: There are many differences related to mentality and cultural backgrounds.

I think that we (in the post-Soviet world) know more about Western humor than the West knows about our humor. Because the Western world was closed to us for a long time, when it opened and all this new TV programming surged into our market, we greedily consumed it and got used to many new things.

However, differences still exist. For instance, gag humor — where you slip on a banana or throw cakes, for instance — isn't really popular in post-Soviet territories. Perhaps that's because such humor is borne from places where people aren't preoccupied with survival. In post-Soviet countries, satire has historically been more popular.

There's also the issue of language: a lot of comedy is built on linguistic forms. Cultural or national backgrounds are important too. Here in Ukraine, we especially like laughing at jokes about relations between in-laws and neighbors.

Still, this gets at a universality to humor. We are all humans, so there must be some common things we all laugh at: family relations, love, children, loneliness. And I feel that even though *Servant of the People* is based on Ukrainian politics, it still incorporates many of these common things.

Q: Let's talk about the elephant in the room: Russia. You and Kvartal 95 first became famous through the Russian game show KVN, and many of your other performances have been quite popular in Russia. At the same time, the "People's President" is known for humorously getting others' attention by shouting "Putin is dead", which probably doesn't make Putin too happy! Are you concerned about losing Russian fans, or do you feel that this is a necessary sacrifice to help Ukraine as a country orient itself towards the West?

A: In an ideal world, I wouldn't want to mix art with politics, even if there's a thematic relation. However, in reality, it's impossible to separate humor itself from politics. Humor must reflect everything that happens in a country, current events and politics included.

Therefore, if today we have complex relations with Russia and a pro-Ukrainian orientation, we must cover all parts of this reality [Russia included]. This is simply an accurate reflection of our society's attitudes, and it's a general world practice. For example, in the US, Trump is President: how can you not talk about it? American shows joke about Trump, and they joke about Russia — though sadly not too much about Ukraine, maybe this indicates we're not so popular!

Now, with regards to our position: I don't put the business first. I believe that first and foremost we are citizens of Ukraine, and we should take care of our country. I think smart people in any post-Soviet country can understand this desire.

Furthermore, the problem of losing fans is mutual [Ukrainians can stop watching Russian-made shows too] [It's important to note that humor is not a personal insult] — I think that people who perceive our humor as a blow in their direction must have an Iron Curtain in their brains higher than the one from the Soviet Union!

Critic review

Cinema Escapist, Anthony Kao, June 6, 2017

If you're looking for great political satire, Ukraine might not be the first country that comes to mind. At the same time, with absurd amounts of corruption and political turmoil, the Eastern European nation provides ample fodder for mockery. As evidence, look no further than *Servant of the People,* a top-notch political comedy that's now silently available on Netflix for global viewers.

Servant of the People (*Слуга народа* in Russian, *Слуга народу* in Ukrainian) chronicles the (fictional) story of Vasily Petrovich Goloborodko, a high school history teacher who suddenly becomes President of Ukraine after a video of him ranting about corruption goes viral. A total political novice, Goloborodko recruits a motley group of friends as his ministers. Together, he and his merry band of reformers use amusingly creative methods to battle Ukraine's entrenched corrupt interests, who respond with their own flavors of dark hilarity.

First released in 2015, *Servant of the People* quickly became one of Ukraine's most popular shows of all time. One contributor to this popularity is the fact that all its episodes are freely available on YouTube (the pilot has 9+ million views) — albeit with English subtitles for only the first two of its 23 episodes.

It was on YouTube that I first discovered the show while preparing for a vacation to Ukraine. After episode two, I was so hooked that I switched on YouTube's automatic Russian to English subtitle translations so I could see more. To my surprise, the show was still pretty watchable.

The fact that I could enjoy *Servant of the People* through the imperfections of machine translation is a testament to its accessibility. While the show was made primarily for Ukrainians, its humor remains quite universal. President Goloborodko is an approachable everyman, a fish out of water whose flopping on land translates well across cultures. He's a President who still lives with his parents, who practices for speeches by stuffing nuts in his cheeks, who wakes up with a hangover after partying with an IMF representative. It's not just Goloborodko though — his family and ministers are equally hilarious, whether his feisty sister or Casanova Foreign Minister.

As such, while prior knowledge about Ukrainian politics certainly makes the show more enjoyable, it's not absolutely necessary. In fact, from a foreigner's perspective, *Servant of the People* is a great way to learn more about the country. Corruption (at least in my opinion) happens to be one of the easiest dimensions through which you can learn about government. After all, greed is universal, and sometimes takes extremely hilarious forms.

On this front, what makes *Servant of the People* far more powerful than any Western comedy is the extent to which its most laughable premises are based on reality. For example,

Goloborodko prepares for his inauguration at an excessively opulent estate, complete with its own ostrich trainer. As it turns out, that scene was shot at the Mezhyhirya Residence, a 340 acre estate — which really has ostriches — built by former Ukrainian President Viktor Yanukovych using public funds. After watching scenes like these, you begin to better understand why Ukrainians overthrew Yanukovych in 2014 and wish that someone could reform their country in the way that Goloborodko is trying onscreen.

Beyond high production quality and a solid story, maybe what makes *Servant of the People* so worth watching is how it embodies the hopes and fears of an entire nation. Three years after the Euromaidan Revolution, Ukrainians in the real world are still waiting for many of the changes they fought for. As they wait, *Servant of the People* helps them glimpse an alternate world, one that they can laugh and dream about. Now, we here in the rest of the world can share in their dream too.

Life imitates art imitates life...

The 'rant' by Zelensky's character in Episode 1 of *Servant of the People*, performed with passionate outrage, which went viral and launched Zelensky's political career:

History teacher Vasily Petrovich Goloborodko (played by Zelensky): *I'm sick and tired of it! I'm done here! Mathematics... is a science! And history is a... shit! And then we are surprised — why do our politicians come to power and make the same mistakes? It's because they are... mathematicians. The only thing that they know is how to divide, add and multiply their own wealth!*

Vasya (a colleague): *Petrovich, I've never heard such language from you in my life. Why did you get so mad?*

Goloborodko: *Because I'm so sick and tired of those... Now they're making the kids build cabins! Do you know why we have a dog's life? It's because we start our choice in the cabins! Do you get it? There is no one to choose! We're choosing between the two... Bastards! It has been like this for 25 years in a row!*

Do you know what is interesting? Nothing will change this time! Do you know why? It's because you, my father, and me will choose a... bastard again! It's because...

"Yes, he is a bastard, but he is still better than the other ones!"

Vasya, let's go and have a drink! I have some left... Then these bastards come to power and steal and steal and steal! These bitches have different names but act in the same way. And nobody gives a shit! I don't give a shit! you don't give a shit, nobody gives a shit! We don't give a small shit, but the shittiest shit in the world!

If I could get there for just one week, I'd show them! I'd do away with their corteges, with the bonuses, with the summer cottages, with all of them!

I wish every common teacher lived like a President! I wish every President lived like a teacher, damn it!

I'm telling this to you like a teacher of history. However, you don't give a shit! Bastards!

CHAPTER 9

THE BUDAPEST MEMORANDUM

In the context of Russia's invasion of Ukraine, Articles 1, 2 and 6 of the Budapest Memorandum clearly provide the US and the UK with legitimate grounds — nay, an obligation — to engage in military action to protect Ukraine. The Russian Federation's violation of this agreement does in no way negate the validity of the agreement on the other parties to it.

It is curious, to say the least, why this agreement has not been invoked by US President Biden and UK Prime Minister Boris Johnson. Indeed, why President Zelensky has not invoked it either?

Preceded by a joint statement demanding the Russian Federation withdraw from Ukraine and a firm deadline, those two world powers would be perfectly justified legally (and morally) to take whatever military action was required to fulfil the terms of the Memorandum.

It is arguable that by failing to invoke the Budapest Memorandum, the US and the UK have not only violated the agreement, they have legitimized the Russian Federation's abandonment of it.

The following is the text of the Memorandum on Security Assurances, known as the Budapest Memorandum, in connection with Ukraine's accession to the Treaty on the Non-Proliferation of Nuclear Weapons, signed December 5, 1994.

The United States of America, the Russian Federation, and the United Kingdom of Great Britain and Northern Ireland,

Welcoming the accession of Ukraine to the Treaty on the Non-Proliferation of Nuclear Weapons as a nonnuclear-weapon State,

Taking into account the commitment of Ukraine to eliminate all nuclear weapons from its territory within a specified period of time,

Noting the changes in the world-wide security situation, including the end of the Cold War, which have brought about conditions for deep reductions in nuclear forces.

Confirm the following:

1. The United States of America, the Russian Federation, and the United Kingdom of Great Britain and Northern Ireland, reaffirm their commitment to Ukraine, in accordance with the principles of the CSCE [Commission on Security and Cooperation in Europe] Final Act, to respect the Independence and Sovereignty and the existing borders of Ukraine.

[Russia has violated this undertaking.]

2. The United States of America, the Russian Federation, and the United Kingdom of Great Britain and Northern Ireland, reaffirm their obligation to refrain from the threat or use of force against the territorial integrity or political independence of Ukraine, and that none of their weapons will ever be used against Ukraine except in self-defense or otherwise in accordance with the Charter of the United Nations.

[Russia has violated this undertaking.]

3. The United States of America, the Russian Federation, and the United Kingdom of Great Britain and Northern Ireland, reaffirm their commitment to Ukraine, in accordance with the principles of the CSCE Final Act, to refrain from economic coercion designed to subordinate to their own interest the exercise by Ukraine of the rights inherent in its sovereignty and thus to secure advantages of any kind.

4. The United States of America, the Russian Federation, and the United Kingdom of Great Britain and Northern Ireland, reaffirm their commitment to seek immediate United Nations Security Council action to provide assistance to Ukraine, as a non-nuclear-weapon State Party to the Treaty on the Non-Proliferation of Nuclear Weapons, if Ukraine should become

a victim of an act of aggression or an object of a threat of aggression in which nuclear weapons are used.

5. The United States of America, the Russian Federation, and the United Kingdom of Great Britain and Northern Ireland, reaffirm, in the case of the Ukraine, their commitment not to use nuclear weapons against any non-nuclear-weapon State Party to the Treaty on the Non-Proliferation of Nuclear Weapons, except in the case of an attack on themselves, their territories or dependent territories, their armed forces, or their allies, by such a state in association or alliance with a nuclear weapon state.

6. The United States of America, the Russian Federation, and the United Kingdom of Great Britain and Northern Ireland will consult in the event a situation arises which raises a question concerning these commitments.

This Memorandum will become applicable upon signature. Signed in four copies having equal validity in the English, Russian and Ukrainian languages.

[Russia has violated this undertaking.]

CHAPTER 10
THE LETTER OF THE WAR

The Russian military chose the letter Z as the symbol for its invasion of Ukraine.

That's a not-too-subtle way of identifying their Number One target: Ukrainian President Volodymyr Zelensky.

The letter started appearing on Russian armour being assembled near the border with Ukraine in mid-February.

Since then, it has been adopted by supporters of Russia's actions, even spawning a merchandising industry within Russia.

There are several theories about the use of Z, the obvious one being the name of Ukraine's resilient president.

Other letters, including O, X, A and V also have appeared. The letters on the hardware were usually framed by squares, triangles, and other painted shapes.

As a letter, Z does not exist in the Cyrillic Russian alphabet and one theory was that Z possibly stood for *Zapad* (west) and the letters being used represented the areas in which the armor was stationed.

Others believe the letters were drawn on tanks and other equipment to try to avoid friendly fire.

The Russian defence ministry did not mention any of the theories but posted on its Instagram channel that Z meant *Za pobedu* ("for victory") and V stood for "power of truth."

Z soon became the symbol of support for Russia's invasion of Ukraine.

London's *Guardian* newspaper reported that just three days after the invasion, state-funded network RT announced on its social media channels that it was selling Z merchandise, including T-shirts and hoodies, to show support.

Some young Russians were seen wearing a Z shirt. The letter also was painted on old Soviet-era apartment blocks and street advertising signs.

The *Guardian* said schools had also posted images of children standing in a Z formation and that one online image showed terminally ill children from a hospice forming a Z to support the invasion of Ukraine.

The symbol has also had some exposure outside Russia. Thousands of Serbs waving Russian flags and carrying Z letters marched through Belgrade to the Russian embassy in a show of public support for Moscow. Russian gymnast Ivan Kuliak had the Z on his uniform as he stood next to Ukraine's Kovtun Illia, the gold medalist at a gymnastics World Cup event in Doha.

It must be noted that support for the Russian action within Russia itself was not universal.

OVD-Info, a voluntary organization that monitors arrests

during protests said almost 15,000 people were detained at rallies across Russia in the first three weeks of the Invasion.

In one demonstration in which 800 people were arrested, a reporter from AFP said some of the riot police had the letter Z in the colors of the Russian flag on their helmets.

Dressed in a yellow hat and blue jacket, 20-year-old Kristina said she was "expressing her protest" by wearing the colors of the Ukrainian flag.

"It's scary to go outside, of course. They are detaining everyone. Lots of my friends have been detained in the past few days, some were even expelled from university," she told AFP.

In a move that would have caught the attention of the viewers of one of Russian TV's most-watched news broadcasts, Marina Ovsyannikova, an editor at state-controlled Channel 1, appeared behind a newsreader holding a sign saying "no war." She also made an anti-war video.

Officials detained her for 14 hours and fined 30,000 rubles ($US 280) for making the video.

In the video, she called on the Russian people to protest the war, saying only they have the power to "stop all this madness."

"Don't be afraid of anything. They can't imprison us all," she said.

Her protest would have been the first time many Russians would have seen or heard the word "war" used in connection with Ukraine.

While the rule requiring Ukrainian men to stay and fight

while women and children fled divided many Ukrainian families, there is division among Russian families as well, between those who backed the war and those who opposed it.

The opinion sometimes seemed to divide along generational lines.

Andrei Kolesnikov of the Carnegie Moscow Center in Moscow said: "In broad terms, younger Russians are less likely to have anti-Ukrainian sentiments. We have seen that the anti-war protests have also largely involved younger people.

"A lot of how you perceive the war depends on where you get your news," he said. "If you watch television, you are simply more likely to toe the official line. And older people tend to watch more TV.

"We see that a majority of Russians appear to support the country's actions, at least the way these actions are presented to them by the media," Kolesnikov said.

It was unsurprising, given the sensitivity of the topic, that the war had created tensions between families and friends: "It is very hard for people to accept that their side are actually the bad guys."

CHAPTER 11

WAR MACHINES: HOW THE ARMED FORCES LINED UP

Ukraine is a military minnow compared to the might of the Russian war machine. David v. Goliath, if you like.

Of 142 countries with ready-to-battle armed forces, Russia ranked No. 2. Ukraine ranked No. 34.

Seemingly running counter to the numbers, it was a surprise when the West learned Russia had apparently sought military equipment from China.

Other US officials said that Russia was running short of some weapons as the conflict dragged on.

But a spokesperson for the Chinese embassy in Washington said the embassy was unaware of any suggestions that China might be willing to help Russia.

"China is deeply concerned and grieved on the Ukraine situation," the spokesperson said. "We sincerely hope that the situation will ease and peace will return at an early date."

The US warned China would face consequences if it aided Russia.

American officials, including White House press secretary

Jen Psaki, have been increasingly critical of Beijing's response to Russia's war in Ukraine.

While Beijing has seemingly tried to strike a neutral tone on the international stage, Chinese domestic media coverage has promoted Russian disinformation campaigns and described the war as a "special military operation," and rarely referred to war.

Psaki also tweeted that Beijing "seemingly endorsed" false Russian claims that the US was developing chemical weapons in Ukraine.

Precise figures are hard to obtain from the countries individually about their armory, but intelligence agencies can make close estimates.

Starting with military spending:

Ukraine's annual military budget is put at $US 5.4 billion (3% of GDP). Russia's is put at $US 61.7 billion (4.3% of GDP). That Ukraine's percentage of GDP is so high likely reflects awareness that the country's neighbor posed a threat.

In terms of boots on the ground, Russia had a massive advantage, although hand-to-hand combat was unlikely to be the way the outcome was decided. Ukraine's active military personnel was put at 255,000 — Russia's at 1,154,000.

With reserve personnel, Ukraine was believed to have 1,149,646 available — Russia 34,765,736.

In terms of Hardware, Ukraine clearly was outnumbered.

Russia had 2,750 tanks ready (18,000 in storage) — Ukraine had 1,150 (1,435 in storage).

Russia had more than 1,500 combat aircraft ready — Ukraine had 139. Poland offered to send its Russian-built fighter planes to the Ukraine air force in exchange for an US supply of its lates fighter planes. The US promptly killed the idea for fear it would be seen by Russia as an act of war.

Russia had around 400 combat helicopters — Ukraine had 139.

Russia had 82 combat vessels — Ukraine had 10.

Russia had around 9,000 units of artillery ready (around 17,000 in storage) — Ukraine had 1,952.

For the invasion of Ukraine, warships and long-range bombing aircraft would not likely be a direct factor.

Ukrainians though were right to fear airstrikes, missile, and rocket attacks. Russia deployed them from the beginning of the action, causing widespread destruction and many casualties.

The Ukrainian military gave stiff resistance to the Russian troops with the new weapons being provided by the West.

Russia

The Russian military used warplanes and Kalibr (Caliber) cruise missiles to attack Ukrainian facilities.

The Kalibr is a precision weapon, with Russia firing them at Ukrainian military facilities and government buildings but also causing civilian casualties.

The Russian-designed Grad (Hail), Smerch (Tornado) and Uragan (Hurricane) multiple rocket launchers also were used to fire a salvo of powerful rockets at troop units or military equipment.

The BM-21 (Grad) is one of the multiple launch rocket systems (MLRS) used by the Russian army. One battalion of 18 launchers can deliver 720 rockets in a single volley. The rockets are unguided and have lower precision than typical artillery; they cannot be used in situations that call for pinpoint accuracy. To destroy a target, they rely on many rockets spread across an area.

Russia has been accused of using cluster bombs in Ukraine. If true, a war crimes prosecution would be likely.

Cluster bombs, also known as cluster munitions, are missiles that explode in the air to release mini-bombs over a large area.

The missiles can be launched from the ground by heavy truck-mounted systems or dropped from planes. But they are often unreliable and many fail to explode, posing a potentially lethal threat to adults and children who find them.

Russia also operates the TOS-1A heavy flamethrower system, a multiple rocket launcher mounted on a tank chassis. Unguided artillery rockets have thermobaric warheads. US defense officials said Russian mobile launchers for thermobaric weapons were seen inside Ukraine, but couldn't confirm their use.

Thermobaric weapons are also known as vacuum bombs because they suck the air out of the lungs of their victims.

A thermobaric weapon explodes in two stages. In the first stage, the bomb detonates, damaging its immediate surroundings with potentially lethal force.

It then releases a cloud of toxic chemicals into the air that can spread into nearby buildings or shelters.

Seconds later, the bomb detonates a second charge that ignites the chemicals, creating a massive shock wave.

This shock wave is capable of vaporizing human bodies.

It also burns up the oxygen in the air, creating a vacuum that can rupture the lungs of people nearby.

International law prohibits the use of thermobaric weapons against civilians, but they are not illegal to use against military targets.

Thermobaric weapons come in various sizes, from rocket-propelled grenades designed for close combat to large versions that can be deployed from planes.

The Russian air force did not have an immediate impact, analysts believing the scale and sophistication of Ukraine's aerial defenses prevented Russia from gaining a foothold with aerial attacks.

Ukraine

The US and Estonia provided Ukraine with Javelin missiles, also known as FGM-148, designed to destroy tanks. They are portable, light and can be launched by one person from the shoulder.

Javelin missiles are designed to hit a tank from above where its armor is thinnest. They have a range of up to 4.5 km (2.8 mi). They can also be effective for attacks on other vehicles, buildings or low flying aircraft.

Lithuania sent Stinger anti-aircraft missiles to Ukraine. The Stinger often is seen as a potential "game changer," giving soldiers on the ground the ability to contest the airspace.

The Stinger's effectiveness was seen in the mid-1980s when Afghan resistance forces used them to shoot down Soviet helicopters. Interestingly some of the first losses by the invading Russians were helicopters, shot down by Ukraine.

Ukraine also had the Bayraktar TB2 unmanned combat aerial vehicle — a Turkish-made drone that can carry small anti-armor weapons.

Ukraine's ambassador to Ankara, Vasyl Bodnar, has said the drones had been very efficient; videos posted by Ukraine's military showed them being used to destroy vehicles in Russian convoys.

The drone can carry small anti-vehicle weapons with laser-guided ammunition.

Sources include CIA estimates, armedforces.eu and reports from websites and other media.

CHAPTER 12
IN THE RED CORNER

Vladimir Putin's disdain for Ukraine that led to the invasion in February 2022 was most likely heightened in 2014 when the pro-Russian government of Viktor Yanukovych was overthrown after months of protests.

Yanukovych fled to Russia and Putin refused to recognize the interim government in Kyiv as legitimate.

Putin got parliamentary approval (possibly to create a sense of legitimacy for what was to come) to send troops to Ukraine to safeguard Russian interests.

By early March 2014 Russian troops and pro-Russian paramilitary groups moved on Crimea, a Ukrainian autonomous republic where the population was predominantly ethnic Russian.

Residents of Crimea voted in a referendum in March to join Russia. In response to the Russian action, Western governments introduced a series of travel bans and asset freezes against members of Putin's associates.

Two days later, Putin, claiming that Crimea had always been part of Russia, signed a treaty incorporating the peninsula into the Russian Federation.

The US and EU further escalated economic sanctions against more of Putin's political allies.

After ratification of the treaty by both houses of the Russian parliament, on March 21 Putin signed legislation that formalized the Russian annexation of Crimea.

Ukrainian regions adjoining Crimea had a significant proportion of Russian loyalists who also wanted to rejoin Russia.

It was probably only a matter of time before Putin took direct action to make that happen. Even though it took him another eight years to make his move, it was no surprise that on February 20, 2022, just before he launched the invasion of Ukraine, that he officially recognized the independence of the separatist Donetsk and Luhansk People's Republics that had been proclaimed in 2014.

The US, UK and EU called Putin's move a "breach of international law."

In a lengthy televised address just before the invasion, President Putin described Ukraine as an integral part of Russia's history and said the areas in eastern Ukraine were ancient Russian lands while modern Ukraine, as a state, was created by the Bolsheviks after the 1917 revolution.

He said he was confident that the Russian people would support his decision.

The Donetsk and Luhansk People's Republics were proclaimed in 2014 when Russian-backed separatists fought

Ukrainian troops in an ongoing civil war.

"I deem it necessary to make a decision that should have been made a long time ago — to immediately recognize the independence and sovereignty of the Donetsk People's Republic and the Luhansk People's Republic," President Putin said.

He also used the speech to attack Ukraine's leadership, saying that neo-Nazis were on the rise, oligarchic clans were rife, and that the former Soviet country was a US colony with a puppet regime.

Whatever Putin's plans were for Ukraine he had plenty of time to enact them. In 2021 he signed a law paving the way for him to run for two more presidential terms, potentially extending his rule until 2036.

Putin, at age 70 in 2022, was in his fourth presidential term that was set to end in 2024. The new legislation would allow him to serve two more six-year terms.

Putin became acting President after Boris Yeltsin's resignation on December 31, 1999. He was then elected President of Russia on May 7, 2000 with 52.94% of the vote, for a four-year term. He was re-elected in 2004, for another four-year term, in 2012 for a six-year term and in 2018 for another six-year term.

Vladimir Vladimirovich Putin was born on October 7, 1952 in Leningrad, RSFSR, USSR (now Saint Petersburg, Russia).

He studied law at Leningrad State University, graduating

in 1975. He worked as a KGB (romanised: Komitet Gosudarstvennoy Bezopasnosti — 'Committee for State Security') foreign intelligence officer for 16 years, rising to the rank of lieutenant colonel, before resigning in 1991 to begin a political career in Saint Petersburg. He moved to Moscow in 1996 to join the administration of President Boris Yeltsin. He briefly served as director of the Federal Security Service (FSB) and secretary of the Security Council, before being appointed Prime Minister in August 1999.

Putin's rule has been characterized by corruption allegations, the jailing and repression of political opponents, the intimidation and suppression of media freedom in Russia, and a lack of free and fair elections.

Putin's Russia has scored poorly on Transparency International's Corruption Perceptions Index, the Economist Intelligence Unit's Democracy Index, and Freedom House's Freedom in the World index.

Putin was married to Lyudmila (now divorced). They had two daughters, Katya and Masha.

It is unclear whether he remarried but his partner is said to be Alina Kabaeva, a 39-year-old Olympic rhythmic gymnastics gold medalist, politician and media manager. They have seven-year-old twin daughters together. It is also believed they have two sons, but their ages and existence have never been publicly verified.

CHAPTER 13
UKRAINE TIMELINE

9th century

Founding of Kievan Rus, the first major Eastern Slavonic state. Kiev became the capital of Kievan Rus.

10th century

Rurik dynasty established, and the rule of Prince Vladimir the Great (Prince Volodymyr in Ukrainian) starts a golden age. In 988 he accepts Orthodox Christianity and begins conversion of Kievan Rus, introducing Christianity in the east.

11th century

Under Yaroslav the Wise (grand prince 1019–1054), Kyiv becomes Eastern Europe's chief political and cultural center.

Foreign Domination

1237–40 Mongols invade the Rus principalities, destroying many cities and ending Kievan Rus's power. The Tatars, as the Mongol invaders became known, establish the empire of the Golden Horde.

1349-1430 Poland and later the Polish-Lithuanian Commonwealth gradually annex most of what is now Western and Northern Ukraine.

1441 Crimean Khanate breaks free of the Golden Horde and conquers most of modern Southern Ukraine.

1648–1657 Cossack uprising against Polish rule establishes Hetmanate, regarded in Ukraine as the forerunner of the modern independent state.

1654 Treaty of Pereyaslavl begins process of transforming Hetmanate into a vassal of Russia.

1686 Treaty of Eternal Peace between Russia and Poland ends 37 years of war with the Ottoman Empire in what became Ukraine and partitions the Hetmanate.

1708-09 Mazepa uprising attempts to free the eastern Hetmanate from Russian rule, during the prolonged Great Northern War that ranged Russia against Poland and Sweden at the time.

1764 Russia abolishes the eastern Hetmanate and establishes the Little Russia governorate as a transitional entity until the full annexation of the territory in 1781.

1772-1795 Most of Western Ukraine is absorbed into the Russian Empire through the partitions of Poland.

1783 Russia takes over Southern Ukraine through the annexation of the Crimean Khanate.

19th century

National cultural reawakening sees the development of Ukrainian literature, education, and historical research. Habsburg-run Galicia, acquired during the partitions of Poland, becomes a center for Ukrainian political and cultural activity, as Russia bans the use of the Ukrainian language on its own territory.

20th century

1917 Central Rada council set up in Kyiv following collapse of Russian Empire.

1918 Ukraine declares independence. Numerous rival governments vie for control for some or all of Ukraine during ensuing civil war.

1921 Ukrainian Soviet Socialist Republic established when Russian Red Army conquers two-thirds of Ukraine. Western third becomes part of Poland.

1920s The Soviet government encourages Ukrainian language and culture within strict political bounds, although this process is reversed in the 1930s.

1932 - Millions die in a man-made famine during Stalin's collectivization campaign, known in Ukraine as the Holodomor.

1939 Western Ukraine is annexed by the Soviet Union under the terms of the Nazi-Soviet Pact.

1941 Ukraine suffers terrible wartime devastation as Nazis occupy the country until 1944. More than five million Ukrainians die fighting Nazi Germany. Most of Ukraine's 1.5 million Jews are killed by the Nazis.

1944 Stalin deports 200,000 Crimean Tatars to Siberia and Central Asia following false accusations of collaboration with Nazi Germany.

1954 Soviet leader Nikita Khrushchev surprises by transferring the Crimean Peninsula to Ukraine. Armed resistance to Soviet rule ends with capture of last commander of Ukrainian Insurgent Army.

1960s Increase in covert opposition to Soviet rule, leading to repression of dissidents in 1972.

1986 A reactor at the Chernobyl nuclear power station explodes, sending a radioactive plume across Europe. Desperate efforts are made to contain the damaged reactor within a huge concrete cover.

1991 Ukraine declares independence after attempted coup in Moscow.

1990s About 250,000 Crimean Tatars and their descendants return to Crimea following collapse of Soviet Union.

A New Beginning

In 1994, Ukraine became the first former Soviet republic to
make a peaceful transfer of power via the ballot box. Leonid
Kuchma won a presidential election, replacing Leonid
Kravchuk.

A new constitution was adopted in 1996, but the
government struggled to implement reforms and the economy
stagnated.

Despite rising dissatisfaction, Kuchma was re-elected in
1999. A protest movement calling for his resignation gained
momentum in the early 2000s.

A presidential election in 2004 showed the pro-Russia
candidate, Viktor Yanukovych, a former governor of Donetsk
region, to be the winner. But evidence of widespread fraud
prompted mass protests in Kyiv (formerly Kiev) which came to
be known as the Orange Revolution and forced a new election.

Victory for Viktor Yushchenko, a political opponent of
Kuchma and former Prime Minister, raised belief that Ukraine
would move its allegiances towards the West, liberalizing its
political and economic systems.

But Yushchenko's reformist coalition lacked cohesion
and failed to implement significant reforms. A party led by
Yanukovych won parliamentary elections in 2006, and after
prolonged negotiations he was named Prime Minister.

Political and economic uncertainty persisted.

In 2009, Russia cut gas supplies to Ukraine amid a dispute

over Kyiv's debt payments. Gas deliveries to many EU states were also affected. In 2010, Yanukovych was elected President and steered Ukraine back towards closer relations with Russia.

He pushed through constitutional changes that enhanced presidential authority and took action to curb dissent. In 2011, Yulia Tymoshenko, a Yanukovych foe and a former Prime Minister, was jailed.

In late 2013, Yanukovych backed away from signing an association agreement with the EU, prompting large-scale protests, known as the Euromaidan movement. In February 2014, Yanukovych fled the capital and was subsequently impeached by parliament.

A pro-western coalition took power. In late February, Russian troops, in unmarked uniforms, moved into the Crimean Peninsula to support local separatists and in March, Russia annexed Crimea, prompting the biggest East-West showdown since the Cold War. The US and European Union imposed ever-harsher sanctions on Russia.

Widespread instability hit eastern regions of Ukraine, as separatist elements, with suspected backing from Russia, took control of several cities and towns. In late May, the pro-West billionaire Petro Poroshenko won a decisive victory in the presidential election, vowing to restore law and order to the East.

War broke out in 2014 after Russian-backed rebels seized government buildings in towns and cities across eastern

Ukraine. Intense fighting left portions of Luhansk and Donetsk, in the Donbas region, in the hands of Russian-backed separatists. The Ukraine Government launched a military operation in response.

Russia also annexed Crimea from Ukraine in 2014.

In July 2014, Pro-Russian forces within Ukraine firing a Russian-made Buk missile shot down Malaysian airline flight MH17 over the eastern Ukraine conflict zone, killing all 298 people on board.

[In March 2022, Australia and the Netherlands — whose citizens were among those who perished on the Boeing 777 — began legal action against Russia over the downing of MH17. They maintained Russia was responsible for the attack and initiated legal proceedings in the International Civil Aviation Organisation (ICAO). They have sought an apology and compensation for the family members of victims.]

In September, NATO confirmed Russian troops and heavy military equipment entered eastern Ukraine.

Parliamentary elections in October produced a convincing majority for pro-Western parties.

In July 2017 Ukraine's association agreement with the European Union was ratified by all signatories and came into force on September 1.

In May 2018, Russian President Putin officially opened a bridge linking southern Russia to Crimea, an action Ukraine called illegal.

President Zelensky

Television comedian Volodymyr Zelensky won a presidential election run-off in a landslide victory over incumbent Petro Poroshenko in April and July 2019.

He took office in May, and his Servant of the People party won early parliamentary elections in July.

In August the Parliament appointed President Zelensky's aide Oleksiy Honcharuk Prime Minister. A month later, Russia and Ukraine swapped prisoners captured in the wake of Moscow's seizure of Crimea and intervention in the Donbas.

In October, Ukraine became embroiled in a US impeachment row over allegations President Trump tried to put pressure on the country over investigating possible Democrat president rival Joe Biden.

In March 2020 President Zelensky appointed former businessman Denys Shmyhal Prime Minister with a mandate to stimulate industrial revival and improve tax receipts.

In February 2022 Russia invaded Ukraine.

Timeline source: BBC

CHAPTER 14

USSR TIMELINE: THE DEMISE OF THE UNION

The Soviet Union (Union of Soviet Socialist Republics, or USSR) was created by Vladimir Lenin in 1922.

It became the largest country in the world.

But after December 25, 1991 the red flag with the hammer and sickle no longer flew on the highest flagpole in the Kremlin in Moscow. Instead, Russia's white, blue and red flag was hoisted in its place.

After its collapse in 1991, the Soviet Union left in its place 15 independent states.

Others opted for complete independence and by the time of the Russian invasion of Ukraine in February 2022 the independent states were Armenia, Moldova, Estonia, Latvia, Lithuania, Georgia, Azerbaijan, Tajikistan, Kyrgyzstan, Belarus, Uzbekistan, Turkmenistan, Ukraine, Kazakhstan and Russia.

The official dissolution of the Soviet Union came on December 26, 1991, officially granting self-governing independence to the Republics of the Union of Soviet

Socialist Republics (USSR). It was a result of the declaration number 142-H of the Supreme Soviet of the Soviet Union that acknowledged the independence of the former Soviet republics and created the Commonwealth of Independent States (CIS).

Five of the signatories ratified it much later or did not do so at all. On 25 December, Soviet President Mikhail Gorbachev, the eighth and final leader of the USSR, resigned, declared his office extinct and handed over its powers — including control of the Soviet nuclear missile launching codes — to Russian President Boris Yeltsin. That evening at 7.32 p.m., the Soviet flag was lowered from the Kremlin for the last time and replaced with the pre-revolutionary Russian flag.

The road to dissolution of the Soviet Union had its origins in 1985 when Mikhail Gorbachev was elected General Secretary by the Politburo on March 11, three hours after predecessor Konstantin Chernenko's death at age 73.

On July 1, 1985, Gorbachev promoted Eduard Shevardnadze, First Secretary of the Georgian Communist Party, to full member of the Politburo, and the following day appointed him minister of foreign affairs, replacing long-time Foreign Minister Andrei Gromyko.

On December 23, 1985, Gorbachev appointed Yeltsin First Secretary of the Moscow Communist Party replacing Viktor Grishin.

On August 23, 1987, the first anti-Soviet protests in

Lithuania took place on the 48th anniversary of the secret protocols of the 1939 Molotov Pact (between Adolf Hitler and Joseph Stalin that ultimately turned the then-independent Baltic states over to the Soviet Union) when thousands of demonstrators in the three Baltic capitals sang independence songs and attended speeches commemorating Stalin's victims. The gatherings were sharply denounced in the official press and closely watched by the police but were not interrupted.

The moves that led to the Soviet Union's demise and independence for the republics continued.

On October 17, 1987, about 3,000 Armenians demonstrated in Yerevan complaining about the condition of Lake Sevan, the Nairit chemicals plant, and the Metsamor Nuclear Power Plant, and air pollution in Yerevan.

On October 21, a demonstration dedicated to those who gave their lives in the 1918–1920 Estonian War of Independence was held in in Võru, which culminated in a conflict with the militia. For the first time in years, the blue, black, and white national tricolor was publicly displayed.

On November 18, 1987, hundreds of police and civilian militiamen cordoned off the central square to prevent any demonstration at Freedom Monument, but thousands lined the streets of Riga in silent protest regardless.

On February 20, 1988, after a week of growing demonstrations in Stepanakert, capital of the Nagorno-Karabakh Autonomous Oblast (the Armenian majority area within the Azerbaijan Soviet Socialist Republic), the Regional Soviet voted to secede and join with the Soviet Socialist Republic of Armenia.

The Estonian Popular Front was founded in April 1988.

On April 26, 1988, about 500 people took part in a march organized by the Ukrainian Cultural Club on Kiev's Khreschatyk Street to mark the second anniversary of the Chernobyl nuclear disaster, carrying placards with slogans like "Openness and Democracy to the End."

The Popular Front of Lithuania, called Sąjūdis ("Movement"), was founded in May 1988. The Latvian Popular Front was founded in June 1988.

In Tbilisi, capital of Soviet Georgia, many demonstrators camped out in front of the republic's legislature in November 1988 calling for Georgia's independence and in support of Estonia's declaration of sovereignty.

On November 16, 1988, the Supreme Soviet of the Estonian SSR adopted a declaration of national sovereignty under which Estonian laws would take precedence over those of the Soviet Union.

In Ukraine, Lviv and Kyiv celebrated Ukrainian Independence Day on January 22, 1989. Thousands gathered in Lviv for an unauthorized moleben (religious service) in front of St. George's Cathedral. In Kyiv, 60 activists met in an apartment to commemorate the proclamation of the Ukrainian People's Republic in 1918.

On April 7, 1989, Soviet troops and armored personnel carriers were sent to Tbilisi after more than 100,000 people protested in front of Communist Party headquarters with banners calling for Georgia to secede from the Soviet Union and for Abkhazia to be fully integrated into Georgia

On April 9, 1989, troops attacked the demonstrators and 20 people were killed and more than 200 wounded. This radicalized Georgian politics, prompting many to conclude that independence was preferable to continued Soviet rule.

On May 30, 1989, Gorbachev proposed that nationwide local elections, scheduled for November 1989, be postponed until early 1990 because there were still no laws governing the conduct of such elections.

In Kazakhstan on June 19, 1989, young men carrying guns, firebombs, iron bars and stones rioted in Zhanaozen, causing a number of deaths.

On June 23, 1989, Gorbachev removed Rafiq Nishonov as First Secretary of the Communist Party of the Uzbek SSR and replaced him with Karimov, who went on to lead Uzbekistan as a Soviet Republic and subsequently as an independent state.

On August 19, 600,000 protesters jammed Baku's Lenin Square (now Azadliq Square) to demand the release of political prisoners.

The Baltic Way or Baltic Chain was a peaceful political demonstration on August 23, 1989. An estimated two million people joined hands to form a human chain extending 600 km (370 mi) across Estonia, Latvia and Lithuania.

On October 28, 1989, the Ukrainian Supreme Soviet decreed that effective January 1, 1990, Ukrainian would be the official language of Ukraine, while Russian would be used for communication between ethnic groups.

On December 7, 1989, the Communist Party of Lithuania under the leadership of Algirdas Brazauskas split from the Communist Party of the Soviet Union and abandoned its claim to have a constitutional "leading role" in politics.

On December 10, 1989, the first officially sanctioned observance of International Human Rights Day was held in Lviv, Ukraine.

On December 26, the Supreme Soviet of Ukrainian SSR adopted a law designating Christmas, Easter, and the Feast of the Holy Trinity official holidays.

On February 7, 1990, the Central Committee of the CPSU accepted Gorbachev's recommendation that the party give up its monopoly on political power.

Gorbachev's decision to loosen the Soviet yoke on the countries of Eastern Europe created an independent, democratic movement that led to the collapse of the Berlin Wall in November 1989, and then the overthrow of Communist rule throughout Eastern Europe.

Gorbachev's decision to allow elections with a multi-party system and create a presidency for the Soviet Union began a slow process of democratization that eventually destabilized Communist control and contributed to the collapse of the Soviet Union.

After the May 1990 elections, Gorbachev faced conflicting internal political pressures: Boris Yeltsin and the pluralist movement advocated democratization and rapid economic reforms while the hard-line Communist elite wanted to thwart Gorbachev's reform agenda.

Gorbachev's domestic problems continued to build. More challenges to Moscow's control placed pressure on Gorbachev and the Communist party to retain power and keep the Soviet Union intact.

After the demise of Communist regimes in Eastern Europe, the Baltic States and the Caucasus demanded independence from Moscow. In January 1991, violence erupted in Lithuania and Latvia. Soviet tanks intervened to halt the uprisings.

On March 17, 1991, in a Union-wide referendum 76.4 % of voters endorsed retention of a reformed Soviet Union.

An unsuccessful August 1991 coup against Gorbachev sealed the fate of the Soviet Union. Planned by hard-line Communists, the coup diminished Gorbachev's power and moved Yeltsin and the democratic forces to the forefront of Soviet and Russian politics.

On June 12, 1991, Boris Yeltsin won 57 % of the popular vote in the democratic elections, defeating Gorbachev's preferred candidate, Nikolai Ryzhkov, who won 16%. Following Yeltsin's election as president, Russia declared itself independent.

Gorbachev tried to restructure the Soviet Union into a less centralized state. A new Union Treaty was drawn to convert the Soviet Union into a federation of independent republics with a common president, foreign policy and military.

On August 19, 1991, Gorbachev's vice president, Gennady Yanayev, Prime Minister Valentin Pavlov, Defence Minister Dmitry Yazov, KGB chief Vladimir Kryuchkov and other senior officials acted to prevent the union treaty from being signed by forming the "General Committee on the State Emergency", which put Gorbachev — on holiday in Foros, Crimea — under house arrest and cut off his communications.

On August 24, 1991, Gorbachev dissolved the Central Committee of the CPSU, resigned as the party's general secretary, and dissolved all party units in the government.

On September 17, 1991, the United Nations General Assembly admitted Estonia, Latvia, and Lithuania to the UN.

By November 7, 1991, the media referred to the "former Soviet Union".

The final round of the Soviet Union's collapse began with a Ukrainian popular referendum on December 1, 1991, in which 90% of voters opted for independence.

On December 8, the leaders of Russia, Ukraine, and Belarus secretly met in Belavezhskaya Pushcha, in western Belarus, and signed the Belavezha Accords, which proclaimed the Soviet Union had ceased to exist and announced formation of the Commonwealth of Independent States (CIS) as a less structured association to take its place.

On December 12, the Supreme Soviet of the Russian SFSR formally ratified the Belavezha Accords and renounced the 1922 Union Treaty.

On December 17, 1991, along with 28 European countries, the European Economic Community, and four non-European countries, the three Baltic Republics and nine of the twelve remaining Soviet republics signed the European Energy Charter in the Hague as sovereign states.

Doubts remained over whether the Belavezha Accords had legally dissolved the Soviet Union, since they were signed by only three republics. On December 21, 1991, representatives of 11 of the 12 remaining republics — except Georgia — signed the Alma-Ata Protocol, which confirmed the dissolution of the Union and formally established the CIS.

They also "accepted" Gorbachev's resignation. While Gorbachev hadn't made any formal plans to leave the scene, he had indicated he would resign as soon as he saw that the CIS was a reality.

In a nationally televised speech early in the morning of December 25, 1991, Gorbachev resigned as president of the USSR.

On the night of December 25 at 7.32 p.m. Moscow time, after Gorbachev left the Kremlin, the Soviet flag was lowered for the last time, and the Russian tricolor was raised in its place, symbolically marking the end of the Soviet Union.

On December 26, the Council of the Republics, the upper chamber of the Union's Supreme Soviet, voted both itself and the Soviet Union out of existence.

Sources: History.com, BBC, Britannica, CBS.

CHAPTER 15
THE ALLIANCES OF EUROPE

NATO

The North Atlantic Treaty Organization (NATO), also called the North Atlantic Alliance, is an intergovernmental military alliance of 28 European countries and two North American countries. NATO was established in the aftermath of World War II, to implement the North Atlantic Treaty, signed on April 4, 1949.

NATO constitutes a system of collective security; its independent member states agree to mutual defense in response to an attack by any external party. It was established during the Cold War in response to the perceived threat posed by the Soviet Union. The alliance has remained in place since the end of the Cold War and has been involved in military operations in the Balkans, the Middle East and North Africa. NATO headquarters is in Brussels, Belgium. The headquarters of Allied Command Operations is near Mons, Belgium.

The admission of new member states has increased the alliance from the original 12 countries to 30.

The most recent member state to be added is North Macedonia on March 27, 2020. NATO recognizes Bosnia and Herzegovina, Georgia, and Ukraine as potential members. Enlargement has led to tensions with non-member Russia. President Putin demanded NATO provide legal guarantees that it would stop expanding east (to countries such as Ukraine, Georgia or Moldova).

The Warsaw Pact

The Warsaw Pact was a political and military alliance comprising the Soviet Union and the communist states of Eastern Europe.

The original members of the Warsaw Pact were the Soviet Union, Albania, Poland, Romania, Hungary, East Germany, Czechoslovakia, and Bulgaria.

The Pact was to facilitate collective decision-making by all its members. In practice, the USSR effectively controlled the organization.

The Warsaw Pact came to an end in 1991, after the collapse of communism in Eastern Europe, and just before the dissolution of the Soviet Union.

The European Union

The European Union (EU) is a political and economic grouping of 27 European countries. The EU promotes democratic values and is one of the world's most powerful trade blocs. Nineteen of the countries share the euro as their official currency.

The EU grew out of wishes to strengthen international economic and political co-operation on the European continent post-World War II. The European Economic Community (EEC), launched in 1957, became the European Union in 1993 with the adoption of the Maastricht Treaty deepening the integration of members' foreign, security and internal affairs policies. The EU established a common market the same year to promote the free movement of goods, services, people, and capital across its borders. A common currency, the euro, was adopted in 1999.

In the 2016 "'Brexit" referendum, the UK voted to leave the EU and the country officially left in 2020.

The Baltic States

The Baltic states — or the Baltic countries — is a modern unofficial geopolitical term for the grouping of three countries: Estonia, Latvia and Lithuania. All three are members of NATO and the European Union.

They are classified as high-income economies by the World Bank and maintain a very high Human Development Index. The three governments engage in intergovernmental and parliamentary cooperation. There is also frequent cooperation in foreign and security policy, defense, energy, and transportation.

The Commonwealth of Independent States (CIS)

The Commonwealth of Independent States, a free association of sovereign states, was formed in 1991 by Russia and 11 other republics that were formerly part of the Soviet Union.

The elected leaders of Russia, Ukraine, and Belarus signed on to a new association to replace the crumbling Union of Soviet Socialist Republics (USSR). The three Slavic republics were later joined by the Central Asian republics of Kazakhstan, Kyrgyzstan, Tajikistan, Turkmenistan, and Uzbekistan, by the Transcaucasian republics of Armenia, Azerbaijan, and Georgia, and by Moldova. (The remaining former Soviet republics — Lithuania, Latvia, and Estonia — declined to join the new organization.) The CIS formally came into being on December 21, 1991 with Minsk in Belarus its administrative center. Today, the CIS states are: Armenia, Azerbaijan, Belarus, Kazakhstan, Kyrgyzstan, Moldova, Russia, Tajikistan, and Uzbekistan.

The CIS Charter was adopted on January 22, 1993. According to the Charter, the goals of the CIS are:

- The members of the CIS would cooperate in political, cultural, economic, environmental protection, and all spheres.
- To promote the economic and social development of all member states.
- To ensure and protect human rights and other fundamental liberties according to international laws.

- Cooperation among all member states for maintaining international peace and security. The Council of Ministers of Defense has been established to coordinate military cooperation among all the member states.
- Prevention of armed conflicts and peaceful settlement of disputes between the CIS member states.

Georgia officially withdrew from the Commonwealth, and on May 19, 2018, Ukraine officially ended its participation in all the statutory bodies of the CIS following Russia's forced annexation of Crimea.

CHAPTER 16

ZELENSKY ADDRESSES US CONGRESS

President Zelensky's historic address via videolink to US Congress (and in the presence of Ukraine's Ambassador Oksana Markarova), on March 16, 2022, was topped and tailed by standing ovations and sustained applause. Will that be the totality of the American response to his call for crucial, lifesaving air cover? He thanked the US for its help to date, invoked history and humanity and he called for a new international institution, the U24, to provide the kind of instant international "police and ambulance" services that existing institutions have failed to deliver.

Zelensky's speech

(Zelensky speaking through an interpreter)

Glory to Ukraine. Thank you very much, Madam speaker, members of the Congress, ladies and gentlemen, Americans, friends. I'm proud to greet you from Ukraine, from our capital city of Kyiv, a city that is under missile and air strike from

Russian troops every day, but it doesn't give up. We have not even thought about it for a second, just like many other cities and communities in our beautiful country, which found themselves in the worst war since World War II.

I have the honor to greet you on behalf of the Ukrainian people, brave and freedom-loving people, who for eight years have been resisting the Russian aggression. Those who give their best sons and daughters to stop this full-scale Russian invasion. Right now, the destiny of our country is being decided. The destiny of our people — whether Ukrainians will be free. Whether they will be able to preserve their democracy. Russia has attacked, not just us, not just our land, not just our cities. It went on a brutal offensive against our values, basic human values. It threw tanks and planes against our freedom, against our right to live freely in our own country, choosing our own future, against our desire for happiness, against our national dreams, just like the same dreams you have, you, Americans, just like anyone else in the United States.

I remember your National Memorial in Rushmore, the faces of your prominent presidents, those who laid the foundation of the United States of America, as it is today. Democracy, independence, freedom and care for everyone, for every person, for everyone who works diligently, who lives honestly, who respects the law. We, in Ukraine, want the same for our people, all that is normal part of your own life.

Ladies and gentlemen, friends, Americans, in your great

history, you have patriots that would allow you to understand Ukrainians, understand us now when we need you right now. Remember Pearl Harbor, the terrible morning of December 7, 1941, when your sky was black from the planes attacking you. Just remember. Remember September the 11th, a terrible day in 2001 when people tried to turn your cities into battlefields. When innocent people were attacked, attacked from air, yes, no one expected it. You could not stop it.

Humanitarian no-fly zone too much to ask?

Our country experiences the same every day, right now at this moment, every night for three weeks now, various Ukrainian cities, Odessa, Mariupol and others. Russia has turned the Ukrainian sky into a source of death for thousands of people. The Russian troops have already fired nearly 1,000 missiles at Ukraine, countless bombs. They use drones to kill us with precision. This is a terror that Europe has not seen, has not seen for 80 years and we are asking for a reply, for an answer to this terror from the whole world. Is this a lot to ask for, to create a no-fly zone over Ukraine to save people? Is this too much to ask? Humanitarian, no fly zone. So that Russia would not be able to terrorize our free cities.

If this is too much to ask, we offer an alternative. You know what kind of defense systems we need. You know much depends on the battlefield on the ability to use aircraft, powerful, stronger aviation to protect our people, our freedom, our land. Aircraft that can help Ukraine, help Europe, and you know that they exist and you have them, but they are on earth, not in the Ukrainian sky. They don't defend our people. "I have a dream." These words are known to each of you today. I can say, "I have a need." I need to protect our sky. I need your decision, your help, which means exactly the same, the same you feel when you hear the words "I have a dream."

Ladies and gentlemen, friends, Ukraine is grateful to the United States for its overwhelming support, for everything that your government and your people have done for us, for weapons and ammunition, for training, for finances, for leadership in the free world, which helps us to pressure the aggressor economically. I am grateful to President Biden for his personal involvement, for his sincere commitment to the defense of Ukraine and democracy all over the world. I am grateful to you for the resolution, which recognizes all those who commit crimes against Ukraine, against the Ukrainian people, as war criminals.

However, now it is true in the darkest time for our country, for the whole Europe. I call on you to do more. New packages of sanctions are needed constantly every week until the Russian military machine stops. Restrictions are needed for everyone on whom this unjust regime is based. We've proposed that the United States sanctions all politicians in the Russian Federation who remain in their offices and do not cut ties with those who are responsible for the aggression against Ukraine, from state Duma members to the last official who has lack of morals to break the state terror. All American company must leave Russia from their market, leave their market immediately because it is flooded with our blood.

Peace is more important than income

Ladies and gentlemen, members of Congress, please take the lead. If you have companies in your district who finance the Russian military machine, leaving business in Russia, you should put pressure. I'm asking to make sure that the Russians do not receive a single penny that they use to destroy people in Ukraine. The destruction of our country, the destruction of Europe, all American ports should be closed to Russian goods.

Peace is more important than income and we have to defend this principle in the whole world. We already became part of the anti-war coalition, big anti-war coalition that unites many countries, dozens of countries. Those who reacted in principle to President Putin's decision to invade our country, but we need to move on and do more. We need to create new tools to respond quickly and stop the war, the full-scale Russian invasion of Ukraine, which began on February 24th, and it would be fair if it ended in a day, in 24 hours, that evil would be punished immediately.

Today the world does not have such tools. The wars of the

past have prompted our predecessors to create institution that should protect us from war, but they unfortunately don't work. We see it, you see it. So we need new ones, new institutions, new alliances, and we offer them. We propose to create an association, U24 — United for Peace, a union of responsible countries that have the strength and consciousness to stop conflicts immediately, provide all the necessary assistance in 24 hours, if necessary even weapons, if necessary sanctions, humanitarian support, political support, finances, everything you need to keep the peace and quickly, to save the world, to save life.

In addition, such associations, such union could provide assistance to those who are experience natural disasters, man-made disasters who fell victims to humanitarian crisis or epidemics. Remember how difficult it was for the world to do the simplest thing, just to give the vaccines against Covid to save lives to prevent new strains. The world spent months, years doing things like that much faster to make sure there are no human losses, no victims.

Ladies and gentlemen, Americans, if such alliance would exist today, that is U24, we would be able to save thousands of lives in our country, in many countries of the world, those who need peace, those who suffer inhumane disruption. I ask you to watch one video, video of what the Russian troops did in our country, in our land. We have to stop it. We must prevent it. Preventively destroy every single aggressor who seeks to subjugate other nations. Please watch the video.

[Short video montage of Ukraine in peace and in war.]

(Zelensky in English) And in the end, to sum it up, it is not enough to be the leader of the nation, it is not enough to be the leader of the world, being the leader of the world means to be the leader of peace. Peace in your country doesn't depend anymore only on you and your people. It depends on those next to you and those who are strong. Strong doesn't mean big. Strong is brave and ready to fight for the life of his citizens and citizens of the world for human rights of freedom, for the right to live decently and to die when your time comes and not when it is wanted by someone else. By your neighbor.

Today, the Ukrainian people are defending not only Ukraine, we are fighting for the values of Europe and the world. Sacrificing our lives in the name of the future. That's why today the American people are helping not just Ukraine, but Europe and the world to keep the planet alive, to keep justice in history. Now I'm almost 45 years old. Today my age stopped when the hearts of more than 100 children stopped beating. I see no sense in life if it cannot stop the death. And this is my main issue as the leader of my people. And as the leader of my nation, I'm addressing President Biden. You are the leader of the nation. Of your great nation. I wish you to be the leader of the world. Being the leader of the world means to be the leader of peace. Thank you. Glory to Ukraine.

(Recorded and transcribed privately on behalf of the authors. E&OE)

The next chapter of this book — indeed, the next book on the subject — will examine the response to Zelensky's moving plea, after the applause has died down.

Andrew L. Urban's first novel, *If You Promise Not To Tell* was nominated in the inaugural Ned Kelly Awards for Best First Crime Fiction. His first non-fiction book, *Murder by the Prosecution* explored several wrongful convictions and was described by Margaret Cunneen SC as a 'troubling expose'. He has published the online Wrongful Convictions Report since 2018. Since 1985, before turning his journalistic attention to miscarriages of justice (prompted by the Eve Ash documentary *Shadow of Doubt*), Andrew was a prolific film journalist and covered the Cannes Film Festival for 20 years for both screen trade publications and mainstream media. He was Channel Host on World Movies for five years. He co-published with his wife Louise, the online movie magazine *Urban Cinefile* for 20 years. During his lifelong career as a journalist, he has had over 2,000 freelance articles published in a variety of publications in Australia and internationally. Andrew conceived and presented *Front Up*, a weekly series on SBS TV that ran from 1992–2003/04. Andrew has profound empathy with Ukrainians: in 1956, with his mother and stepfather, he fled from Russian tanks during the Hungarian Revolution.

Chris McLeod is a former newspaper journalist and executive. He was Foreign Editor and News Editor at the *Newcastle Morning Herald* and News Editor at the Melbourne *Herald*. He is an author and researcher for floggerblogger.

com with an interest in sport, transport and mystery. His bookazines include *World's Best Golf Courses*, *World's Best Trains*, *Elite Special Forces* and *Unsolved: Terror Crimes and Accidents*. He is the co-author of *Barty: Arise, Queen of Oz*.